START
TO GROW...
AGAIN

**REBUILDING YOUR BUSINESS
WHEN IT ALL HEADS SOUTH**

All rights reserved
Copyright © Philip Bain, 2020

The right of Philip Bain to be identified as the author of this
work has been asserted in accordance with Section 78
of the Copyright, Designs and Patents Act 1988

The book cover is copyright to Philip Bain

This book is published by
Grosvenor House Publishing Ltd
Link House
140 The Broadway, Tolworth, Surrey, KT6 7HT.
www.grosvenorhousepublishing.co.uk

This book is sold subject to the conditions that it shall not, by way of
trade or otherwise, be lent, resold, hired out or otherwise circulated
without the author's or publisher's prior consent in any form of binding or
cover other than that in which it is published and
without a similar condition including this condition being imposed
on the subsequent purchaser.

A CIP record for this book
is available from the British Library

ISBN 978-1-83975-240-7

CONTENTS

SECTION ONE
SURVIVING AND GROWING IN A CRISIS

3-6 /   **INTRODUCTION**

7-26 /   **START TO...RESPOND TO THE CRISIS**

- 9   Get a grip on the situation
- 10   Make decisions for the immediate
- 11   Make decisions for the next few weeks
- 13   Get on with running the business
- 14   Ongoing communication
- 15   A strategy for the next couple of quarters
- 17   Avoid all immediate instincts – they won't work!
- 20   Reflect on fundamental truths – this will work!
- 23   Check out if your business is still relevant

27-43 /   **START TO... REFLECT ON THE CRISIS**

- 29   Go for a walk to get clarity
- 33   The Five R's of recovery
- 38   Start to...get back your turbo
- 42   Reflect on new opportunities

45-90 /   **START TO...REBUILD THROUGH THE CRISIS**

47	Start by confronting the brutal facts...again!
53	Start to establish an advisory board
58	Start to get a business advisor to join the board
67	Leading people by doing the right things
74	Build up your Wisdom, Knowledge and Discernment (WKD)
76	Start to do *some* innovation
81	Start to do *more* marketing
86	Start to get *hold* of the financials

SECTION TWO
MENTORING AND PUBLIC SPEAKING

91-106 /   **START TO...MENTOR OTHERS**

93	Introduction
97	What mentoring role to adopt?
98	Identifying a mentee
100	Mentoring is essentially about finding solutions to problems
102	The Mentoring Dynamic

107-152 /   **START TO ... DO PUBLIC SPEAKING**

109	Introduction
110	Let me tell you my story on the public speaking thing
114	To speak or not to speak, that is the question...
116	Understanding the brief

118	Putting your presentation together
122	Preparing your presentation
125	Day of the presentation
127	Delivering the presentation
132	How to engage the audience!
144	Talk killers
146	Things to avoid
148	Give people a road map to success
150	Some final tips...
152	Give them a message of hope

SECTION ONE
SURVIVING AND GROWING IN A CRISIS

INTRODUCTION

INTRODUCTION

I'm writing this when the stats look ugly. Everything you read and hear is quantitatively terrible. I read that the economy may be tanking by 30% and I hear of another brutal heart wrenching number on daily death toll. US unemployment numbers reads close to an entire working population of a medium sized industrial nation! The world is on pause and slipping silently into a very dark place. And yet my instincts remain strangely positive. And the reason for my positivity is because of my habit of defaulting to the fundamentals.

And the fundamentals are that mankind will always need something to survive and want more to thrive. And the way to get our needs and wants met is either to kill or trade. Opting for a less catastrophic option, I optimistically land on trade as the natural human instinct in order to survive and thrive. Therefore, if trade is here to stay in some shape or form then we already start with an optimistic brick on the foundations of recovery. As we start to build confidence that mankind will always trade, then what do we now need to do when everything around us is on the descent including our own business that we love and cherish? What is our response to a crisis of incalculable consequences that goes beyond even the most pessimistic of risk scenario planning?

Well that depends. It depends on you. Will you take advice? Will you change? Will you reach out? Will you do what this book says? I've had people throw my books into the corner of the room (a guy actually did that!) when a sentence or two like that cut deep or just hacked someone off. This may be a throw it in the corner moment but can I suggest a moment of restraint. At the heart of revival in anyone or anything is humility. In other words, are you coming at this with humility and a realisation that reaching out, listening to others, and seeking help is the starting point in this? I have reached out many times and conversely metaphorically thrown the book in the corner and tackled the storm on my own…badly. I have learnt from painful experience that the bridge from crisis to clarity is to cry out to someone other than yourself. And, sure, when you do get advice coming your way there will always be the need to separate the stinky stuff from the shinola but let's hope you can get some shoe polish from this book to help rebuild your business in the midst of the calamity.

I am convinced that my calling in life is to lead in times of crisis. I don't do calm …I get bored anyway and although crisis pushes you to the limits in every sense it is a heck of a lot better than the dull predictability of calm. My previous books share my personal story of my father's business collapsing in the midst of a global recession and eye watering interest rates and at the same time being diagnosed with leukaemia.

I watched a fighter (and in my view the best) take the world on and rebuild his health, his business, and his financial fortunes by bringing the Pizza Hut franchise to Northern Ireland when we didn't even have a McDonalds! Some fathers teach their sons football, mine taught me business. No one motivates me but he does. Whatever the world threw at him, he had a deal, he had a way around it, he had the thing sorted.

Over the years, I personally have dealt with rescuing a business that had run out of cash the day I walked through the door to manage it, led another business through the calamity of tripling its turnover in a few weeks after securing a major contract, grew our business with my business partner James through the global credit crisis and subsequent great recession, and in parallel with all this had to deal with a range of complex and serious challenges in leadership in other realms outside of business. At one point, I was involved in the leadership of 19 entities at one time and although some of them had huge, and sometimes painful, challenges I loved it. It's what I do and as I say, it is my calling.

My father saw business as a game and in my view, you have to love it to play it well. If business is something you "like" you probably won't survive – you have to love it! At the time of writing we are in the biggest business challenge of our lives – we all are. That's the game we are in now – some will choose not to play it and give up but you – yes you, are not one of those people. You love it, so let's get out and play the game like we have never done before!

I have written a book called "Start to Grow" which covers business start-up and growth and another book called "Start to Lead" that covers leadership. Both of these books cover a huge amount of what you need to do to start up, grow and lead a business in all circumstances. However, we are really in unchartered territory as I write this book and my business partner and I felt that there was a need for a complementary book to "Start to Grow" and "Start to Lead" given the economic circumstances we are in. The book will explore how we respond to a crisis largely in the short term (up to six months) and then the other books kick in and complement after that. The book will also look at evolving the leader/business owner to a mentor and thought leader who can communicate his/her story on stage. There's a lot to chew over and don't miss the "5% trick" later on in the book – it's a good one!

Anyway, when the whole economy was nose diving, in a moment of trying to bring a little humour to an otherwise desperate situation, I jokingly texted my business partner James:

"I've an idea for a new book – Start to Grow…again!"

James got the joke but brought up a month later

"I knew you were joking but it's a good name for a book."

And the rest as they say….

Enjoy and be well ☺

SECTION ONE
SURVIVING AND GROWING IN A CRISIS

START TO... RESPOND TO THE CRISIS

WHATEVER THE CRISIS AND WHENEVER IT COMES, HERE ARE SOME THOUGHTS ON HOW WE SHOULD RESPOND IN THE SHORT TERM:

GET A GRIP ON THE SITUATION

The immediate thing is to understand what has happened and what is happening with your business and the world around you. You need to understand what the true nature of the crisis is and the impact it has had on your business and is likely to have in the coming weeks.

Action: Following on from my previous books, information is vital for the leader. At the macro level, you need to watch the news, read the papers and become informed as to what exactly is going on. At this stage there is going to be a lot of noise around you – there will be theories, uninformed chatter and opinion, emotions running high and all of this, like it or not, will start to form our thoughts and reactions. To avoid this, seek the facts of the matter from various informative sources. Also, at the micro level, start to build a picture of how your business is being affected by getting an immediate grip on the key numbers re cashflow, sales, costs etc. Head in the sand stuff just won't work!

MAKE DECISIONS FOR THE IMMEDIATE

Based on the information that your business has been severely impacted by a crisis - the longer you procrastinate the more consequential and deeper the damage will be to the business. The immediate decision however, may be "wait and see" and this can be a wise and sensible approach. I remember as a kid watching a coup in Russia that ousted the current leader and I remember the American President at the time taking a relatively calm "wait and see" approach. The coup fizzled out and the world didn't descend into Armageddon. Wise move Mr. President!

Action: Knee-jerk reactions can be highly consequential, so be careful. However, sometimes decisions need to be made, so, at this stage, there are simply going to be the things you can influence and the things you can't influence. Focus on the things you can influence to protect the business. At all times seek alignment and consensus across the business and particularly with your senior managers/partners/fellow directors. Being of one mind at this time is vital! Ongoing communication with staff is essential in moderating fears and bringing as much clarity as you can.

MAKE DECISIONS FOR THE NEXT FEW WEEKS

Your immediate responses and decisions have ensured that all that can be done to stabilise the situation has been actioned. You now need to think a little into the future. At this stage, as the picture of what is going on in your business and the world around you is emerging, you can now at least make an educated stab at what needs to be done in the coming weeks.

Action: At this stage do nothing revolutionary or make a significant strategic pivot to a different business model! For the next few weeks, you need to think more tactically to ensure the business is on a sound footing. The main focus at this stage will likely largely be around operations and administration to ensure that the business can still function effectively and efficiently delivering that same promise to the customers that made your business what it is today. Contracting your cost base and cutting your cloth to the new reality will be obvious moves for you to make and sadly those moves may be largely forced on you anyway. It goes without saying that all the normal rules still apply regarding cost cutting – just because it is a crisis it doesn't mean that you abandon all the rules of the game. There must be in all decisions – buy in and alignment, sound decision making based on data and not emotion, adherence to good practice and legal compliance etc.

GET ON WITH RUNNING THE BUSINESS

There is a brutal reality here that no matter what is going on in the world and how calamitous the situation is – if your business is still relevant and it is still viable and the shutter doors are still open, then life has to continue.

Action: Your business may have experienced a 70% contraction in turnover or have a catalogue of challenges and barriers you never experienced before. However, if you can still function then your business has to continue delivering that same amazing customer experience that you have always delivered.

ONGOING COMMUNICATION

Keeping everyone in the dark is disastrous and ultimately counterproductive. Fear and uncertainty will undoubtedly be amongst the people around you but it will be intensified by no communication. And communication must also be to customers, suppliers, shareholders and other relevant stakeholders. Everyone in your world needs to know what is going on, your response and how that impacts on them.

Action: The key thing is to keep everyone updated by state of the nation addresses and one to one discussions in order to bring assurances if assurances can be given, to bring hope if hope exists and indeed to show that as a leader you are on it, you understand it and you are making the best decisions to keep the business moving forward. If required, correspondence to customers, suppliers and other key stakeholders in order to communicate to them the current state of your business, what plans you have in place going forward and the impact on them.

A STRATEGY FOR THE NEXT COUPLE OF QUARTERS

Three-year plan and five-year plans – forget it! The situation is just too volatile at this stage. Your business is in A & E, maybe even critical care and you have experienced a battering that goes beyond the normal rough and tumble of business life. Therefore, you can only really think the next couple of quarters. The key thing is to set out very achievable realistic goals for the next three months that include sales, profit and financial numbers that work and are achievable. We are talking about gradual recovery and not some defibrillator electric shock treatment activity. The slow and achievable, steady as she goes quarter will allow some rebuild in the morale of the staff, a time of healing on the accounts and some reflective strategic thinking for the future.

Action: Everyone will have different decisions to make but the key things to think about are to ensure that the business isn't haemorrhaging cash, costs are under control, the business is restructured accordingly to ensure that the business can survive. See what is available to you in terms of government grants, low interest loans and other forms of business support. At this stage everything has to be data driven and not emotionally driven. And although we have to think in the next couple of quarters, we still have to think long term strategically. And what I am getting at here is that you may have to make severe cuts as a business but it is important you don't cut too deep into muscle that will ultimately impede recovery when recovery comes. For example, if you remove certain people from the business to save money in the short term, you may be impeding recovery because the business will lack certain skill sets that will be required when everything begins to normalise.

AVOID ALL IMMEDIATE INSTINCTS – THEY WON'T WORK!

- **Instinct one – Rediscover the young buck from the past**

    There may be an immediate sense that we have to reach back into the annals of time to bring back the young buck in the organisation (either you or someone else significant) who had bags of energy and ruthlessness and whose passion propelled the business miraculously and spectacularly into growth levels unseen in years. If you recover that person, then the world will be won again.

    From the get go let me make this very clear - that person is gone, but even if you could get him or her back you wouldn't want him or her now. Yes, there was energy in that person and yes, there were guts but perhaps not a lot else! That person ten years ago was ten years less experienced, less smart, less knowledgeable...no, leave him or her there in the past! That instinct won't work.

- **Instinct two - Diversify or Die**

    "Diversify!!" "Create a new business!!" "We need to pivot!!" "Pivot...pivot we need to pivot!!"

Ok, relax please! Yes, diversify and yes, create a new business but I guarantee whoever is propagating this strategy wants it done on a shoe string budget, taking only 20% of their time and probably very little of existing staff's time, and delivered on a sheepish marketing budget approach. Nope! That won't work! I've tried it in the past and it just does not work. You know and I know if you want to create a business then it is a rocket to the moon herculean effort of money, energy, zero return for three years, and all hands to the wheel effort. Diversification is no different than any business start-up and it requires exactly the same ingredients. And if you are up for that - sure - create one business, heck create two or three of the businesses! However, know that for diversification to work and be successful, it means doing the whole thing over again and all of that is covered in my first book – "Start to Grow"!

- **Instinct three – Cut, cull and kill**

  The instinct is to slash the budgets like a crazed axe murderer (metaphorically speaking). Now is the time to cut the deadwood, "that wee so and so who I've been eyeing up for months, even years, is now going to get the proverbial chop!" That marketing budget that you thought was over bloated and self-indulgent, you are just chomping at the bit to pull it apart. This is the time to gain total control over the budget so you can completely and justifiably, because of the current circumstance, wield the powerful axe through the organisation. And yes, there may need to be a bloodbath – the key numbers that are staring back at you on screen may dictate it and that is it! The point I'm making though is "motive." If the cuts are thought through, strategic, and part of an overall plan of restructuring and renewal, then of course do what needs to be done. However, if the motive is driven by all the wrong things – like revenge, frustration, fear, bias etc, then don't do it. I'm of the rather mystical view that a business is like a living being – it has in a sense, a soul, a character, a personality. Before you wield the axe, and you may well have to, remember you will not just remove a budget or a person, you will remove something deeper and intangible that you may never be able to get back. If you cut for cutting's sake, then you are going to damage the soul of the business.

- **Instinct four – Consider this to be "the big one"**

We all are kind of waiting for the big one! The seismic event that will change everything in our business and the world around us. Those "big one" events have happened in the past like The Great Depression, the invention of the printing press and discovery of penicillin, WW1 and WW2 etc. These events really did change everything. And yes, the crisis you are going through now may well be one of the historic pivotal moments. It may be - but then again it may not be. Just remember the whole thing may just revert back to largely the way it was, or a version of it. Only time will tell if it is the big one or not – but don't waste too much time trying to determine that. We all just have to run with what we see and know at the time.

REFLECT ON FUNDAMENTAL TRUTHS – THIS WILL WORK!

- **Fundamental truth 1 – Trade is not dead**

  If trade dies, then that is it – the whole party is over! Have you ever watched Mad Max movies? If trade dies then it's Mad Max time – sand dunes and sandals, shooting people for fuel and food, a lawless and destitute world! That's clearly not where we are at right now because you wouldn't be reading this book – you would be out scavenging the highways for food! So, knowing that trade is not dead, then hope springs eternal and our business can survive and indeed thrive in a world where people still trade. The market may have changed or is changing and consumer buying patterns and tastes may be moving in a different direction, which may mean your business has to adapt and adopt a new approach but the key thing is that trade is alive and opportunities still exist for your business.

- **Fundamental truth 2 – There are many levers available to pull**

  Sometimes when a crisis comes, you feel totally powerless. Essentially you are like a stationary person stuck on a moving walkway – moving in one direction with no power to get off, move away, change the speed or direction of travel. And this is simply not the case. You have a whole bunch of levers to pull. You can speak to your bank and have a conversation about increasing your financial levers through having access to a greater breadth of facilities to help cashflow. You can pick up the phone and ring 100 companies and see if they want to buy your stuff – no one is going to stop you! You can reduce overheads by easily 5% across the board – it may be painful but it is a lever you can pull. In reality, you will find you are not as powerless as you think. You have a lot of levers that you can pull that will bring your business forward.

- **Fundamental truth 3 – Things haven't stopped, they are moving really fast**

  There's a myth during times of crisis that everything is on pause mode. Actually, this is complete nonsense. Everything is moving at an incredible pace. What do I mean….as you stare out the window with a tumbleweed passing by? Well, anything that was heading up the growth side of the curve like tech, renewables, pharma etc will be accelerating exponentially and anything that was already on the slow descent of the curve will be heading nose dive like a stray meteor passing through the world's atmosphere. Everything is moving fast and that pace presents great opportunities for the smart business to leverage.

- **Fundamental truth 4 – Your business model can be changed**

  What, change my business model? Never! You may have to! In challenging times, you have to take the business model down from the shelf, dust it down, hold it in your hand and check it out. Now the business model might be dead and if so, bury it and don't try and resuscitate. However, you might find that the old thing still has life in it yet and still remains relevant. There may be a need to adapt, change, refine and innovate how you do things but the business model is largely still relevant. Doesn't matter what's going on in the world – if your business model is still relevant, then you are still in play!

CHECK OUT IF YOUR BUSINESS IS STILL RELEVANT

No matter how interesting or innovative your product is, how nice your beautifully decorated retail outlet is, or how comfortable your leather sofa in reception feels, if your product or service does not provide a solution to a problem, then your business will never survive. Fundamentally, you need to again ask yourself the following questions:

- **What problem does your product/service solve?**

  Business is about problem solving. If you solve problems for people, then you have a strong chance of succeeding even in challenging economic times. The great news is that there is never a shortage of problems in this world. There are problems everywhere, and people will always pay to get the big ones sorted. So, you need to make sure that you identify a problem that already exists and know that your product uniquely solves that problem. Otherwise, what is the point?

- **Does the problem exist in sufficient numbers?**

  There may be a problem out there that you have identified but if there is only one business or one person wanting the problem solved, then there is no business opportunity. You have to ask yourself the question – Are there enough people out there suffering the problem, that your business can solve? This is your market research; take a fresh look at whether your solution is still required in sufficient numbers to make your business sustainable and profitable. The economy could be booming but if your solution is simply not needed in sufficient numbers, then your business will collapse.

- **Do people want a solution?**

There may be sufficient numbers of people with a particular problem and they may need a solution to that problem. However, you need to identify if they actually want a solution to that problem. Some people are happy to endure the problem. There are a lot of problems that we face every day, but on many occasions, we simply don't want, or are not prepared to pay for a solution. If you have the problem of being overweight, there are obviously many diet and exercise solutions out there. The diet or exercise program provides the solution to the problem; the end result may be great, but many people just don't want to sign up to it. We maybe don't like sitting in traffic on our way to work, but are we prepared to have that problem solved by paying £500 for a helicopter to take us instead? Okay, that may be an extreme example, but life could be made easier and problems could be solved by money or by changes in lifestyle, but on many occasions, we are simply not prepared to pay for those solutions. The solution has to be desired, and people must be prepared to pay for that solution to make your business viable.

- **Will the price paid be less than the cost of enduring the problem?**

Following on from the previous point on whether people are prepared to pay for the solution, the next fundamental question you must ask is whether the price you charge is less than the cost of enduring the problem. For example, I live on the top of a hill in the country, surrounded by fields, trees and cows, which is great, but unfortunately, I cannot get high-speed broadband. I was told a couple of years ago that the solution to that problem would cost me £100 per month. At that price, I would rather just live with the problem of slow connection, even though I do want the solution. For now, anyway, the price of the solution is more than the cost of enduring the problem so, for me – no sale.

- **Why would people buy from you?**

So, we have established that your business still solves a problem and there are sufficient numbers of *problem suffering* people out there to make your business still viable, but why would those customers buy from you? What is it about your business and your products or service that compels individuals to bypass your competitors and purchase from you? This is something that requires much thought so consider your answer carefully, but whatever you do, please, please, please don't say "because we give a good service". Everybody says that and in the customers' eyes, that is not enough.

- **Will the end result be beneficial?**

The couple who enjoy a delicious meal at a great restaurant see the end result as "a wonderful experience". These customers are likely to bring repeat business and become 'ambassadors' for the brand to their friends and family because they have benefitted from the excellent customer experience provided by the restaurant. Will the end result for your customer be beneficial? Will their quality of life have been enhanced after encountering your service? Will they have saved money? Will they have a more efficient business? When the deal has been done, will the customer have experienced a tangible, beneficial result from doing business with your company? If there are a lot of people out there suffering a problem and they want a solution and you can provide that solution with the end result being beneficial to them, then you are in the game.

SECTION ONE
SURVIVING AND GROWING IN A CRISIS

START TO...
REFLECT ON THE
CRISIS

GO FOR A WALK TO GET CLARITY

A nuclear bomb has hit your business. The world is collapsing around you. Emotions are through the roof in you and others. Uncertainty reigns and chaos is everywhere. You need to get out of that environment! Every decision you make at this point is tainted by emotions, clouded by fears, and distorted by the fluid nature of circumstances. The thing you need to do is get away from it all and start to walk so that you can think and reflect without distraction or distortion. Part of the process of growing again is reflection. And reflection does not happen in a context of noise – it is in the quiet place. And often that quiet place can only be found in walking.

As you walk, you need to think about what is actually going on. What are the issues as you see it? What are the problems that need to be sorted? What solutions are available to you? Thinking time is so necessary to ponder over what's happening and reflect over the issues in order to start to formulate rich insights that will make you start to sketch out a way forward. Walking brings clarity, it opens your eyes and it gives you insights to the real truth of the matter. Let me share this with you…

One of my favourite films ever is a 1980s comedy movie called Ferris Bueller's Day Off. It's a film about a guy who skips school for the day to show his friend a good time by walking him around Chicago. They eat in a fancy restaurant, watch the stock market, go to one of the world's tallest buildings, view an art gallery, drive a fast car and watch the ball game, all in one day!

I read recently, however; the deeper meaning of the film was that Ferris actually took him to Chicago to rescue his friend from suicide. He wanted to show his friend that life was still worth living by showing him what the world has to offer – art, trade, sport, fine dining, architecture, city life, music, and the value of friendships.

Over the hundred times (literally) I watched the film, I had missed the deeper meaning. This wasn't a film about a guy just selfishly having a fun day and getting his friend to tag along, this was a film about a young man who made a selfless act to save his friend (if Ferris was caught by the crazy headmaster who was pursuing him – he would not graduate). Yep, 100 times watching the film and I missed the real meaning!

Interestingly, at the beginning and end of the film Ferris looks at the camera and says "Life moves pretty fast… if you don't stop and look around once in a while you could miss it." Life does indeed move pretty fast. We are consumed with doing our jobs, managing our businesses, reacting to stuff that comes at us and pushing forward our own agendas and plans. With all this activity, we do miss a lot. We miss what's really going on below the surface with people that are close to us and with people we don't even know. And maybe we also miss what's really going on with ourselves.

So, it seems to me that one way to get a deeper sense of it all is to stop everything, put your coat on (because it's usually pretty cold out there) and start walking. It will take a bit of time but you will start to do something we rarely do – you will "think" and then you will do something even rarer – you will "reflect." And as you think and reflect you will start to observe the world around you. You will see things you have never seen before in yourself and others, you will get clarity on stuff that has been to date confusing, and perhaps you will also have conversations with strangers that will give you rich insights and perspectives that will help you, and others, on the journey. Then, you may start to have deeper conversations with those who you normally only engage with at the surface level.

I recently did an evening walk around Belfast. What did I see? I saw the usual busy rush of people coming and going, some great buildings, and some amazing food. However, look a little deeper under the surface and it takes you to a different world; a homeless girl who looked not much older than my young daughter, a business owner who behind the jovial trader was a guy struggling to care for his sick wife and his son who also has his major struggles, a young guy who just left his home in England with the hope of turning a hobby into an enjoyable enterprise, and a homeless man on the street who has no hope other than the possibility someone would dare to treat him as a human being, even for a brief moment.

On that walk of thinking, reflecting, observing and conversing, I easily learnt more in two hours than the last six months of just "doing." As Ferris Bueller says… "Life moves pretty fast…if you don't stop and look around once in a while you might miss it."

Therefore, in preparing for growing again, go out and start to walk and by thinking, reflecting, observing and just enjoying pure silence, you will start to formulate thoughts, ideas, action points, and insights that will give your understandings of the situation and the way forward with greater depth and meaning than you ever thought possible.

THE FIVE R'S OF RECOVERY (RECOGNISE, RISK MINIMISE, REMOVE, RESTORE AND REFOCUS)

RECOGNISE

There needs to be recognition of what is actually happening in the business and to truly take stock of where the business stands. Has the crisis led to your market contracting irreversibly and if so, to what extent? What state are your finances in and what are the projections for the next couple of quarters? Is the competition stronger or weaker as a result of the crisis? What opportunities exist, if any, and what threats do we need to be conscious of? There needs to be a proper sit down with the key people in the business to figure out exactly the state of the business…. good, bad and ugly. Recognise also opportunities that exist to adapt and change in order to respond to the crisis in a way that enables the business to not only survive but thrive.

RISK MINIMISE

The general view that entrepreneurs or business owners are risk takers, is one of those inaccurate myths that can often be peddled out in seminars, lectures and text books etc. Risk taking in the classic sense of the word is throwing the family silver on red and hoping the crazy risk will pay off! Entrepreneurs and business owners (the good ones anyway) are actually not this type of risk taker. Instead, they are risk minimisers. To use an awful business term – they are people who "de-risk". They are always trying to "de-risk" the many risks that exist in their world.

One of my earliest business lessons from my father was "protect the downside and the upside will look after itself" (I didn't have an ordinary childhood where my father and I talked about football scores!). Great business people and highly wealthy ones will of course take risks, and the wealthiest will usually take the greater risks, but built into their risk strategy will be risk minimising or de-risking. For example, de-risking may be bringing in a brilliant Human Resource person and paying them above market rate in order to minimise the risk of poor HR policies and practices that could lead to costly unfair dismissal claims, tribunals and high staff turnover. Also, de-risking may involve raising money for a new venture through the use of angel investors or venture capital firms rather than risking your financial security by using your own personal money or borrowing against your house. We de-risk for example by investing in marketing to reduce the risk of losing market share, or by having comprehensive insurance policies over and above the minimum required, just in case something goes badly wrong.

As business people we like to think of ourselves as risk takers - it sounds more heroic, entrepreneurial, and adventurist. However, in reality, we more often than not default to de-risk. We may of course take high stake risks from time to time but the general trend for those who survive and thrive in business is that consciously or subconsciously, we are in the business of de-risking.

Don't engage in high stake risk strategies in times of crisis. Don't do some stupid tech pivot costing you a fortune and sinking the whole ship. The strategy for surviving a crisis is much more mundane in reality. Seek to be de-risking in everything you do. You want to close off all your vulnerabilities, build walls in the weak parts of the fortress and strengthen the line. This does not mean that you should not be thinking investment, creativity and innovation in all areas in the business, but it will be done in the context of risk minimising. For example, you may need to invest several million to upgrade your plant and machinery. This sounds risky financially (and at one level it is) but it actually is risk minimising in that it ensures that the organisation can deliver products more efficiently, cost effectively and at a quality that surpasses the competition, and this will ensure that the risk of losing market share to competitors is perhaps not eliminated but the risk is definitely minimised.

REMOVE

What are the barriers to moving forward? What needs to be removed in the business in order to move forward? Maybe it is the overdraft limit that needs to be removed to be replaced by a higher limit to give you financial resources to move forward. Maybe it is a staff member who needs to be removed because they are not with the programme of renewal. Maybe what needs to be removed, is marketing activity that doesn't provide return and quite frankly never did. Maybe it is the removal of a whole bunch of assumptions that we have about the business that we never tested. Look at what needs removing to move forward and take the hard, and maybe sometimes easy, decisions to do what needs to be done to grow again.

RESTORE

What needs to be restored that to date has been ignored? What processes have you stopped using for months and even years? Maybe you had a slick system of standard operating procedures that everyone used to adhere to, but as time went on the systems have degraded with growth in sales having covered a multitude of sins. It may seem a bit secondary but actually this point is fundamental – restore all the good systems and processes to ensure that you are able to deliver a consistent above average customer experience to all your clients.

There also may be restoration of old marketing initiatives that used to work quite well but over time you got bored with them, but in reality, they were really good for the business. Maybe start cold calling again! Yes indeed – that old fashioned sales approach may just be what is needed to grab some market share. Maybe reactivate the customer relations programme or corporate hospitality activity that everyone got bored with and felt had burnt out. These things may no longer be relevant but don't be afraid to dust off some old books and see whether they are still a good read or not.

REFOCUS

Having recognised what is going on in your business and the world around you, and having adopted a sensible de-risk strategy, then having removed all barriers and restored all that was once good but had degraded over time – now is the time to refocus.

And what do I mean by refocus? Refocus on growing your business and achieving goals that you have set. Those goals may have had to change and be refined but make sure you have agreed goals going forward and that your team are all of one mind on those goals. And it is important, as you know, to have a clear strategy on how those goals are to be achieved.

START TO...GET BACK YOUR TURBO!

A crisis can batter you mentally, emotionally and physically. You may feel like quitting and throwing in the towel. That is understandable but the reality is that you have to keep going and you have to keep pushing forward. The following is a real-life story I told recently in my blog which resonated with a lot of people. It was titled "Getting back your turbo."

A couple of weeks ago, late one evening, my car broke down. The engine computer reported 34 faults! I managed to get the car going again to get home but it was driving very sluggishly, as it had gone into "restrictive performance". The following day I went to the car service department - it was like driving on second gear all the way to Belfast! However, for anyone looking at the car, as I drove down the road, everything would have seemed normal - it was driving on the correct side of the road, going at reasonable speed, looking reasonably clean, and doing what it was meant to do. However, the reality was, that despite appearances, the car was massively underperforming because the service team told me that the turbo had broken down. This didn't happen instantly - I was informed that the deterioration had been going on for some time.

Now here comes the parallels!! Sometimes we can lose our "turbo." In other words, we lose our ability to high perform. We lose our energy and passion and the consequences are we no longer have the power to do the things necessary to stay competitive and ahead of the game. Creativity can go, enthusiasm for chasing new customers can burn out, and the ability to perform to deliver exceptional results may no longer be in our capability. This doesn't happen overnight, this deterioration will have been going on for some time. Through the course of things, you, or your business, have suffered highs and lows, bumps on the road and plenty of complex challenges. All this takes its toll. And if that has happened to you - here's what you need to do to get back your turbo.

GET IT FIXED

The first simple step is to recognise the turbo has gone - the passion and enthusiasm, the energy, the clarity of thought are all operating at restrictive performance. All recovery starts with recognition. If you recognise it, you will want to fix it. And to fix the problem you need to reach out to someone who will mentor you by helping you identify areas in your life that need changed.

CHALLENGE YOUR ASSUMPTIONS

We live by a whole bunch of assumptions that we have made over the years. We make assumptions such as "I need to work 60 hours a week", "I can't delegate tasks", "I have to continue doing this or bad things will happen", and "if I don't do it no one else will" etc. These assumptions may or may not be true. One way or the other, they need challenged, refined and changed. Get a mentor to do this with you. The end result will be action points to start making changes that will allow you to offload things, make changes, reprioritise, and get some energy and clarity back into your world.

LOOK AFTER YOURSELF

The turbo in my car didn't break down for no reason. It had broken down because I had forgotten to service the car and had not given it any love and attention.

It takes a bit of discipline to give yourself attention but do a few simple things; like go to bed an hour earlier, eat less rubbish and take a walk every so often. Also, go out with a friend for a laugh and a chat a bit more regularly than you are doing. You should also play hard to balance things off. For me playing hard is taking hotel breaks and eating ridiculous amounts of Reese's American chocolate - but each to his/her own!

KNOW YOUR PURPOSE

A car's purpose is pretty clear - to transport me from one place to another safely, comfortably and maybe with a bit of style. What is your purpose? For now, just forget goals and targets and all that stuff - it's probably all those unrealistic targets that contributed to you losing your turbo in the first place. Instead, get laser clarity on what your purpose is, and then focus on only those things that enable you to deliver that purpose. And stop doing things, for now, that are not relevant to your purpose.

So, recognise you need to fix the turbo, get someone to help you do that by challenging the assumptions you live and breathe by, refine and change those assumptions, take some rest and eat well, and recapture your purpose.

You are now on a journey to getting back your turbo!

REFLECT ON NEW OPPORTUNITIES

Naturally our instincts are to see threats everywhere and opportunities nowhere. However, there are opportunities! And there will always be opportunities:

- **Opportunity to grab market share**

  The pie may be getting smaller but there is an opportunity to get a bigger slice. Many of your competitors may go under and others may not respond in the right way. For you and your business, there is an opportunity to grab more market share and acquire market leadership or indeed strengthen your existing market leadership.

- **Opportunity to get great marketing deals**

  In times of crisis you don't want to exploit anyone or anything but there are deals to be had in the marketing sphere. Set a budget and negotiate hard for deals in advertising, direct marketing, digital etc. I've covered this before in my previous book "Start to Grow" – be really aggressive on the marketing front in times of crisis as it will pay huge dividends in the medium to long term.

- **Opportunity to be part of the solution**

    There are great opportunities to be an organisation that is part of the solution to the crisis. Bold initiatives in corporate social responsibility that involve giving of a service free, giving financially, giving of time, volunteering etc. Think of ways that you can give back and help the world that is burning around you.

- **Opportunity to think differently**

    There is an opportunity to think differently about everything. Start to think how you can do things smarter, more efficiently, more creatively. Think of ways you can adapt and change to the world around you to remain relevant and continue to grow.

- **Opportunity to be more profitable**

    Let's be honest, there are moves that you want to make and in reality, need to make concerning the business. That may be the cutting of an unprofitable division, the ending of an inefficient process or the taking out of certain people through redundancy. Now is the time to get the thing really profitable by moving on stuff that, in reality, you just couldn't really do in the past!

SECTION ONE
SURVIVING AND GROWING IN A CRISIS

START TO...

REBUILD

THROUGH | **THE CRISIS**

START BY CONFRONTING THE BRUTAL FACTS...AGAIN!

During challenging times, when it all starts to go wrong and when deals are being lost, clients are leaving, and service levels are patchy and when the days of everything you touch turning to gold are a distant memory, what do you do? How do you respond to this slump? What do you do when things are going wrong in your business, when staff are just not as enthusiastic anymore and when life is just no longer as fun as it used to be?

First of all, this is common. It is, as they say, the stuff of life. Things start, things grow, things decline regardless of what is going on in the economy. People change, the environment changes, and you change. Things are but for a time and then change happens. It is inevitable. So what do you do to a business that is spiralling downwards, that is starting to look and feel like the businesses you once made mincemeat out of? Your response is to first of all understand what is happening. The heart of the problem sometimes can be the problem of the heart! What is going on at the heart of your business?

To understand this, you need to start by confronting the brutal facts. Good sales performance in a business can cover a multitude of sins. When times are good and profits are being made and all is well in the world, there are many underlying issues and problems in our business that we simply don't deal with. We don't deal with them because, well, we don't need to. Or we think we don't need to! The underperforming sales rep isn't removed, the inefficient process is tolerated and the unprofitable product line is ignored because to confront these problems can be too painful. The business does well despite these problems and, to use that terrible line, "we just kick the can down the road," to be dealt with another day, or not, if we can avoid it. Many business leaders naturally shy away from painful experiences and prefer to focus on the good stuff. Many years ago, my old boss used to always ring me before a board meeting and say, "what good news do we have for the board?". There was a stack of bad news that needed to be dealt with, weaknesses that needed to be addressed, threats that had to be countered, but he didn't want to talk about any of that and he assumed, I think wrongly, that the board didn't want to talk about it either.

In my view, good news will take care of itself, it's the bad stuff that won't and it is the bad stuff that can ultimately destroy a company. During times of plenty, we can feel that we have the luxury of being able to ignore these internal business weaknesses because, we think, "Hey, we are making money, so why rock the boat?" However, when times are tough and the business is facing difficult challenges, we must confront brutal facts about the underlying weaknesses within our business.

In my mid-twenties, someone was good enough to hand me the reins of a start-up and give me my first general manager role. Inexperienced and seriously lacking in more areas than I have time to mention, my role was to grow the business and to bring energy to this fledgling start-up. The company had enjoyed a reasonably good few contracts to kick-start the business and I was there to add more to the pile and of course, deliver them for the clients. However, as I was soon to discover, adding contracts and generating sales is only one part of creating a sustainable business. Three weeks into the job, I was sitting in the lofty heights of one of my three offices enjoying all the trappings of a young general manager, and my finance manager walked into my office and told me, "the cashflow has hit a brick wall and we can't make payroll."

The realisation that I was actually responsible not only for sales, but the livelihoods of all my staff suddenly hit me. There were salaries to pay in a couple of weeks and there was no money to pay them. For the next two weeks, I had to confront the brutal facts about the business. Sales were not enough, the business needed more. It needed good banking facilities, it needed efficient systems and processes, and it needed credit control and tight cash flow management and there were also too many mouths to feed! These weaknesses all needed to be confronted and dealt with. This was a painful experience but necessary. The comfortable position the organisation had enjoyed up to that point was gone and everything now had to change. Over the next few months, the business became more effective in cash flow management, contracts were delivered on time and on budget, but many tough decisions had to be made.

Dealing with problems, making painful changes, dumping unprofitable contracts and having difficult conversations with staff is not something I relished and

I suspect I am not the only one. If you are the type of manager or leader who comfortably confronts long-standing issues and problems in an organisation, then save yourself more time and flip to the next section as you have mastered something many have not. If you are like me, keep reading.

The starting point in overcoming the challenges of growing your business during a recession is to confront some brutal facts about you and your organisation. To do that, we have to ask ourselves four very simple questions:

1. **What is the business good at and how can we repeat it?**

   Over the last 12 months, what area has the business performed well in? It could be that your business is great at securing new contracts or that you are managing your cashflow well. Whatever it is you are good at, write it down and then focus on how you are going to repeat it. The key thing is embedding that 'good thing you do' in the organisation to ensure that it is not dependent on an individual or group of individuals who may leave the organisation.

2. **What is the business bad at and how can we stop it?**

   Over the last 12 months, what has your business performed badly in? It could be that your business is bad at credit control or your customer service has become inconsistent. Whatever it is you are bad at, write it down and focus on how you are going to sort the problem out. The key thing is to address 'why' it is happening and to look at the root cause of the problem rather than just tackle the more obvious 'what' is going wrong.

3. **What product, process or person is preventing success and what are we going to do about that?**

   This may be obvious or it may require some searching. One thing is guaranteed, if you are not growing or you want to grow more, then you have to address anything that is preventing your business moving forward. We avoid confronting these weaknesses for understandable reasons. We can be emotionally attached to a process that is inefficient because, well, we created it. We ignore an unprofitable product line because our customers like it, and we can keep hold of the wrong person because they have been there from the start and have always been loyal. Our inertia is understandable but we have to move on it!

4. **What product, process or person is driving success and what are we going to do about that?**

   This again may be obvious or it may require some searching. There are key employees, profitable product lines and slick processes that all 'just work'. What is the reason for their success? Why are they working so well and how can we make the whole organisation just as good? Beyond that, how do we make sure all those good people stay and keep performing, those processes keep efficient and that product remains profitable? All these issues have to be addressed.

These questions are designed to confront the brutal facts about your business. They have to be answered honestly and the issues have to be addressed with urgency. There may be an argument, perhaps a weak argument, for 'head in sand' mentality during the boom periods but when we want to grow our business during challenging economic conditions, we must deal with the internal weaknesses in our business. Let's face it, we can't do anything about the external factors impacting on our organisation, so we might as well focus on the things that we can change!

START TO ESTABLISH AN ADVISORY BOARD

The challenges in times of deep economic crisis are nothing short of enormous. Seismic reductions in turnover, enormous financial strains and the picture rapidly changing minute by minute is the reality of the moment. And for such a time as this you need to build an "advisory" board. You may employ three people or three hundred people – it doesn't matter – form an "advisory" board. Having chaired four boards and been a non-executive director on six I know all the issues with "boards" so hold fire on the cynicism for a moment. It fundamentally is about bringing key people together to help you – that's it. And you do need help – everyone does.

THE COMPOSITION AND FUNCTION OF THE BOARD

The board should meet initially two-weekly. It should consist of directors/owners and possibly key staff members. Outsiders should include someone to advise on marketing (maybe your designer or digital marketing support person), your accountant should be there and ideally an independent chairman. The meeting should essentially be about bringing in a strategic approach and response to the crisis with real time unemotive information to guide decision making. The meeting should have an agenda, minutes taken, and it should be a strong accountability and challenge function to the owners and directors. This board will allow the space and bring in the expertise to think and reflect on ways that the business can innovate and adapt to changes, ways in which the business can be more efficient, and a forum to stimulate new ideas and strategies going forward.

THE ADVISORY BOARD SHOULD CHALLENGE ASSUMPTIONS

We all live by a bunch of assumptions. And if you are a leader, you and others within the organisation are going to have a bunch of assumptions that individuals, teams and the organisation have. Those assumptions could be around the quality and capability of certain people, the profitability of certain products, the effectiveness of a marketing activity and indeed the list is endless. All of these assumptions that you and others hold could indeed be true, or they could be false, or there could be a mix of assumptions that are bang on true and others that are complete nonsense. The advisory board should start to challenge assumptions and to get people to think rather than feel. Assumption challenging should not just be done by the board or the leader but you should encourage this practice across the organisation.

Assumptions need to be challenged and the answers to those challenges cannot be emotional responses, or "this is the way we have always done it" responses, or generalisations. When challenged about assumptions, the reply answer has got to be based on data. Assumptions need to be challenged and responses have to be data based.

Often, assumptions will be proved wrong as people see the reality of the data before them. A business owner who assumes they are profitable can quickly see that assumption smashed by monthly management accounts, properly presented and explained by a good accountant. We assume perhaps that we are great leaders but that assumption can be blown out of the water by organisation wide employee feedback. Assumptions are like beliefs - we hold them dear to our heart. However, they can be wrong and the problem with wrong assumptions is that they are the foundations for our actions and behaviours. Wrong assumptions will lead to wrong actions and behaviours. Therefore, the advisory board needs to break wrong assumptions, get to the truth of the matter and change actions and behaviours for the better.

THE ADVISORY BOARD SHOULD STRENGTHEN THE ACCOUNTABILITY AND CHALLENGE FUNCTION

Human nature is what it is – flawed, very flawed! And we all need boundaries and parameters in our world in order to keep us focused, effective, and to avoid drift. At every stage in the organisational journey there should be a strong accountability and challenge function. Everyone needs to be held accountable for the role that they have and they are tasked with fulfilling. It is every leader's responsibility to ensure that whatever environment he or she is leading there must be an accountability and challenge throughout the organisation.

- Accountability

    The leader should ensure that everyone has formally been given the expectations of their role, the requirements, anticipated outputs, and targets. The leader should ensure that people know what is expected of them in the organisation. Leadership needs to make sure they have formal conversations setting out those expectations. Then leaders should revisit that discussion every six months (or whatever frequency they think necessary) in order that there is no confusion or misunderstanding. The people should know clearly what they need to be delivering. And it is also important that everyone has the training, tools, resources and guidance to deliver on those expectations.

Secondly, the leader should be encouraging a clear understanding of implications of delivering or under delivering. People should understand very clearly what happens, both positive or negative, if they exceed expectations or under perform. That should be clear to everyone and there should be no misunderstanding.

In a company I used to work for, there was a target for the sales reps that had to be achieved within three weeks of starting their job. They knew what it was, they were given the tools to achieve it, but failure to achieve those sales results led to instant dismissal. It may seem harsh but everyone knew what was expected (realistic or otherwise) and they knew the consequences if it wasn't achieved. No surprises and no awkward conversations.

- Challenging

    People need to be held accountable but also challenged to continue to develop and grow. Everyone needs to be challenged about their performance, challenged to train more, learn more, and be more creative or whatever you feel they need to focus on in order to better achieve the goals.

Challenge should be peppered with encouragement and support, affirmation and confirmation of their strengths and successes. And whatever you are challenging them on, it has to be directly linked to the overall goals of the organisation.

You may challenge them about their aloof personality or weird dress sense (probably better not doing this!) but neither of these may be relevant to their ability to achieve goals for the organisation.

Challenge on areas that are relevant and that are necessary, making clear that it is for their betterment, and the betterment of the organisation as a whole. Make sure they know and understand that - and it is not challenging for challenging's sake.

START TO GET A BUSINESS ADVISOR TO JOIN THE BOARD

Let's start with the obvious. A business advisor is an individual who provides advice to an individual, group or organisation either on a paid or unpaid capacity. The person could be an experienced business professional who advises based on their own personal experience. The person could be relatively inexperienced in business but can offer specific business advice on a particular specialism (e.g. quality systems, IT, HR policies) because they are highly trained by a multinational consultancy organisation that also supports the advice process with the rigour, resource and processes that add value to the client. The business advisor may be a generalist and advise on everything from the price of beans in Burma to the best way to sell snow to the Eskimos! Alternatively, the business advisor may be a specialist in a particular area like marketing or HR and they have developed this specialism over many years as a practitioner and advisor.

Essentially a business advisor is typically someone from outside the organisation and, through their high level of Wisdom, Knowledge and Discernment (WKD), delivers solutions to problems to an individual, team or organisation. Problem solving is at the core of the business advisor's engagement with the client.

The business advisor may engage in an informal unstructured approach by providing advice from time to time and when issues arise. And also, the business advisor can be engaged on a more formal, regular basis and charging fees for their time.

WHAT DO BUSINESS ADVISORS BRING TO THE TABLE?

Business advisors can often arrive into an organisation to help "fire fight" or resolve certain issues that have just become insoluble problems that have perhaps started small but have become systemic in the organisation and are impacting negatively across certain areas. When trouble comes and you are in the thick of something pretty big, then it may be worth considering an advisor to help.

Here is what a business advisor can bring to a crisis:

- They are not in the weeds…

    Sometimes when you are immersed in a problem and down in the weeds, it is very hard to look at a problem objectively, unemotionally and with clarity. A business advisor has the benefit of coming at problems with greater objectivity, emotional detachment and clarity of thought. The business advisor is not weary from the battle and caught in the emotion of it all.

    Note to business advisor - make sure you keep it this way because it is always very easy to get drawn into the battle and down in the weeds. Your value is not being in the weeds so don't devalue yourself by heading for the weeds!

- Experience

    Very few paths have not been trodden on and the likelihood is that a business advisor will have trodden quite a few paths, and maybe even created a few new paths themselves! Issues around dealing with a crisis, implementing organisational change, dealing with office politics, management issues, managing underperforming sales people etc. are all familiar stuff to the seasoned business advisor.

    Note to business advisor - take all the good and bad experiences of your personal journey and share that wealth of experience to help the client fix things, avoid pitfalls and also maybe just feel OK about the fact that bad stuff happens. Sometimes tell stories to contextualise the advice but don't tell too many stories of past heroic leadership because it gets annoying!

- Specialism

    Most business advisors tend to have one thing that they are really good at. A business advisor may be great at organisational change, or operations, or finance, or marketing and business growth. A business advisor is able to add value by bringing their wealth of experience and understanding on a particular area of business. This specialism, that the business advisor is advising on, will likely be an area that the organisation is weak in. And that weakness is likely to have a strong negative impact on the business moving forward.

    Note to business advisor - in a rapidly changing world, make sure you remain subject matter expert

in your specialism. This is what sets you apart and you don't want your knowledge in this area to degrade and devalue because of a failure to continuously learn and develop.

- Adult in the room

    Sometimes things can get a bit out of hand. People start behaving in a childlike manner. A childlike manner is manifested in childlike behaviours in that people become very emotional, matters are less about facts and more about feelings, issues are not addressed and if they are addressed, they tend to be done through gossiping, "telling on others", and being argumentative. Childlike behaviour is also people struggling to take ownership of situations and constantly passing the buck to the next tier up. And in this scenario a business advisor comes in out of the cold and is the adult in the room.

    Note to business advisor – be the adult. Approach the situation with maturity, with authority and with behaviours characterised by the very opposite of the childlike behaviours that I have just outlined. And indeed, a business advisor should encourage adult-like behaviour across leadership and the organisation as a whole!

- Broader picture

    It is hard to see the broader picture at times, but I like to think of myself as a broader picture type of a guy! We can focus on particular short-term issues that are impacting on the organisation and it can get us down and worried and wearisome. However, sometimes it is good to gaze around and see the bigger picture that the organisation has a lot of positive things going on.

Note to business advisor - it is important to sort out the short term, immediate problems but it is also important that you get people to see the bigger picture whether positive or negative.

- Facilitating, not doing

    The business advisor can often find themselves doing some of the heavy lifting and doing things for others. This sometimes is necessary, unavoidable and in fact, it may even be good practice if it is around for example an HR issue. However, the primary role is to facilitate change and to facilitate others to do the work that needs to be done.

    Note to business advisor - make sure that you are advising, empowering, encouraging, developing, and guiding but try and avoid too much "doing". The "doing" is for the people in the organisation!

- Ownership

    A really good business advisor should have a sense of ownership of the organisation that they are advising. They should like the people and like the organisation – maybe even love it! There should be a sense of really wanting to see the organisation or the individual doing well and going forward and having issues resolved etc. There should be an emotional dimension to the engagement and not simply a cold engagement to get a fee.

Note to business advisor - strike a good balance between emotional detachment and objectivity, and a strong sense of ownership and emotional commitment to the folks that you are trying to help move things forward.

- More thinking and less feeling

    People are quick to lose it and go off the handle. Everyone is emotional, and to be a bit Orwellian about it, some are more emotional than others. Complex situations, times of crisis and conflicts can make some people react in irrational ways. They lose their cool. It is the only way they can respond. However, the knee-jerk reaction and the emotive behaviour more often than not typically inflames the situation and generally creates more heat than light! I know, I have done it many times to my regret.

    However, a great business advisor is someone who reacts very differently. A business advisor is calm. While everyone around is jumping up and down, screaming and over-reacting (for undoubtedly legitimate reasons), the business advisor is the calm and tranquil head. Why? It's simple. That's the trait of a great business advisor. The reason why great business advisors keep calm is simple – they are not subject to his or her emotions or governed by them.

    Note to business advisor - you need to be characterised by self-control. You need to be the calming influence on a dynamite situation. With this inner calm and control of one's emotions, the realities don't get clouded and you can then be focused on what the true issue in the room is. And that is a true mark of a great

business advisor – someone who quickly gets and focuses on the *issue in the room*. You will more clearly see the issue, how to resolve it, and then what needs to be put in place to prevent a repeat. Business advisors are not out for blame, although heads may roll, but rather, they are focused on ensuring the environment achieves its goal - nothing more and nothing less.

- Strategic thinkers... tactical believers

    Business advisors think strategically but also believe fundamentally in the importance of tactical decisions. They are "big picture" people through and through. The immediate issue or action is of course of interest, but of greater importance are the consequences of that immediate issue or action on short, medium, and long-term goals.

    Note to business advisor - your thinking should be: "What is the impact of that decision on the long-term goals of the organisation?" As you stand at the foot of the mountain, you should see the tactical challenges of the rocks, boulders and brutal weather but you should be more focused on looking at the top of the mountain, the opportunities of climbing the mountain, and the potential opportunities that lie beyond it.

"Known knowns", "known unknowns" and "unknown unknowns"

The former United States Secretary of Defence, Donald Rumsfeld was asked a question at a U.S. Department of Defence (DoD) news briefing on February 12, 2002 about the lack of evidence linking the government of Iraq with the supply of weapons of mass destruction to terrorist groups. Rumsfeld stated:

"Reports that say that something hasn't happened are always interesting to me, because as we know, there are known knowns; there are things we know we know. We also know there are known unknowns; that is to say we know there are some things we do not know. But there are also unknown unknowns – the ones we don't know we don't know. And if one looks throughout the history of our country and other free countries, it is the latter category that tend to be the difficult ones."

We all have a bunch of stuff we know we know – "known knowns." For example, in business **we know we know** how to deliver a great customer experience and sell our products. However, there is also equally a bunch of stuff that **we know we don't know** – "known unknowns." For example, we perhaps **know we don't know** about how to develop and implement a digital marketing strategy or how to scale our organisation for growth through restructuring. And then there is a large chunk of stuff that **we don't know we don't know** – "unknown unknowns." For example, at the time of writing in 2020, Covid 19 was very much in the realm of unknown unknown. This is the stuff that you can't plan for, that you can't get advice on, and has the potential to have a major impact on you and your business both positively or negatively. Unknown unknowns can be technological changes that can wreck or enhance your business, a new competitor that comes out of nowhere, or it may be simply ignorance to financial management that could have a negative impact on your business.

The stuff we know we know (known knowns) is not what we need a business advisor for. You don't need to pay someone to advise you on what you know. You are, as they say, "on that!" However, the stuff that we know we don't know (known unknowns) is where external business advice could be useful. A business advisor can only really add value to a client when you advise them on matters that they don't know. For example, the client may want to achieve a quality standard and require advice on implementing standard operating procedures, or the client may be in an employment dispute and need specific HR advice.

A really good business advisor will also be about reducing the stuff that we don't know we don't know (unknown unknowns). A business advisor should not just be about giving advice on the specifics of the problem, but the advice should also be about building knowledge with the client so that they will start to learn new things, build awareness in areas that they never even considered, and therefore start to reduce the stuff they don't know they don't know (unknown unknowns).

Therefore, if you are getting a business advisor, then get straight to the "known unknowns" and determine if they add value by turning these matters to "known knowns." And, then seek to build knowledge and understanding to help reduce the "unknown unknowns." Know what I mean?

LEADING PEOPLE BY DOING THE RIGHT THINGS

My book "Start to Lead" covers a good chunk of leadership, so I am going to try and avoid duplication. In times of crisis or in times of calm, I contend that my definition of leadership still stands – "creating an environment that enables goals to be achieved." As a leader you are always, and will always be, in the business of creating an environment of infrastructure, people, organisation and culture in order to achieve whatever goals have been set. However, in the outworking of leadership here are some thoughts on doing the right things and how you should be with people…whatever happens.

- **Build Trust**

    If people don't trust you, then they will not open up and the relationship is doomed to failure. Trust comes from simply being trustworthy. Make sure you never share with anyone what they share with you – no matter what! Make sure you deliver whatever you promise to those you lead and make sure you never give cause for them to mistrust you.

- **Build Respect**

    You must have the utmost respect for those you lead. Respect their position, respect their thoughts and views, respect them in how you converse with them and conduct yourself with them. In all matters, respect the relationship and respect the person. Disrespect in any form is wrong and also will have the potential to break the relationship. And of course, it goes without saying that respect goes both ways in the relationship.

- **Be Honest**

    There should be honesty in every sense of the word. You should encourage others to be open and honest and you in turn should be honest in everything you say. There should be honest speaking on both sides. Everyone needs to hear the truth – warts and all. As their leader, you need to be honest about their weaknesses and shortcomings, areas that need addressed, and perhaps perceptions that need to be changed. Honesty should always be gracious but sometimes you need to be brutally honest in order to bring home to others the really important areas that need addressed. Like most things in life, balance is key! It is best that brutal honesty is mixed in with encouragement!

- **Be Gracious**

    Grace is a huge word that in many ways is undefinable. By simple definition, grace is unmerited favour. Being gracious is showing favour, care and love to someone regardless of who they are, what they have done and how they even behave towards you. Regardless of people's mood, and regardless of their attitude and regardless of their behaviours – good or bad – always determine to be gracious in your dealings with people.

- **Be Discerning**

    Discernment is the ability to determine truth from error. The ability to discern comes from building up knowledge and wisdom. Discernment is a rare gift but a powerful one that enables the one who possesses the gift of discernment to cut a straight path through all the emotion, fluff, and words, to get to the truth of the matter. Discerning people can be scary enough as some people don't always want to share the truth, the whole truth and nothing but the truth – but discerning people will see the truth no matter how hard you may try to hide it. Therefore, build discernment so that you can always see the truth of the matter. You can then address the true issue and take things forward for the people you lead.

- **Be Non-judgemental**

    Judge not lest you be judged. We don't like to think of ourselves as judgemental but one way or another we judge people based on what we consider to be the infallible standard – our standards. And we can't do that. We are not in a position to do that and have no right to do it – a judge has that right but not us!

- **Be Humble**

    Be humble. The point about humility has been made in this book and my previous books. We don't have all the answers and there are plenty of imperfections in ourselves and as leaders we need to convey that in every sense of the word. Pride is destructive but humility brings great gain for you and others. If you are humble, you hopefully will encourage others to be humble. And the principles of a humble spirit will be the desire to ask for help, surrounding yourself with those who are better than you and drawing on their strength as they draw on yours, and also to be comfortable with your own weaknesses. If you make people comfortable with their weaknesses, they will be open about them, they will share those weaknesses with the leader and they will be relaxed about talking about them and how they impact on their life and possibly the lives of others.

- **You are not human**

    As humans we are not perfect. We are weak and therefore have weaknesses. We have vulnerabilities. There are patterns and practices in our lives that may be dysfunctional, questionable, and unhealthy. Do people need to know this? Do they need you to share this? In my view, no they don't. The leader needs to be a giant, a hero, someone to look up to and not one who spills their guts out about their weaknesses and vulnerabilities. The purpose of leadership is to help others, to be a role model and to encourage others on their journey. If it is a friendship, then that's perhaps different – let them see your weaknesses, your fears and your vulnerabilities if you want. Be human with friends. But as a leader - be a little less human!

- **Sometimes listen...don't speak**

  There is a time to just shut your mouth – and this is not easy for anyone never mind someone who is trying to lead through a crisis.

  A GP told me recently that they are being taught more to listen to the patient and let them speak more. Apparently, this approach has improved accuracy in diagnosis and the direction of travel for the patient's health significantly. Seems obvious to encourage others to listen but it may be, in many ways, a dying art. Let's face it – how many people out there are actually listening? Do politicians really listen to what the public are saying? Do business owners really listen to their customers or their staff? I mean, we hear what they are saying of course but as a good friend of mine said to me recently over an egg McMuffin... "yes, you hear me but are you listening!?"

  Typically, an entrepreneur and/or leader is just full of experience and knowledge that is just pouring out of them and the tendency is just to talk, advise and cut to the chase. However, discipline yourself. Listen...and listen...and listen a bit more. Data collect, ask questions and build a picture and then move forward.

- **The answer does not always lie within**

  I have no thorough understanding of coaching. But the essence of it seems to be that the answer to problems lies within you. The coach just needs to get it out of you. Granted, the answer may lie within the person or people that you are leading and for some emotional, mental or intellectual reason, they need that support or stimulus to get at the solution. That is not always the case...sometimes people just don't know and they will never know the answer until someone advises them with the suggested course of action. And don't say "this may work" ...the bloke off the street could give you that advice. You have to say this will work because experientially you know it to be true. There should always be allowance for the unpredictable and uncontrollable variables that could prevent the advice working but all things being equal, this advice is good and it works.

- **Love, care, carry....**

  I find it hard to say to anyone other than my wife and kids that I love them. It's not that I don't love other people, it's just saying you love someone has all the dangers of being misconstrued ...and anyway, words can be largely irrelevant. It is the actions that will determine the degree of love that someone has for you. People can judge accordingly. The word "love" has been misused and misunderstood which has led to all sorts of problems. So, what is "love?" Love is sacrifice – plain and simple. The degree to which you love someone will be seen in the degree of sacrifice that you make for that person. It's quite scary when you think about it. If you subscribe that love is less about the emotions, less about the physical, less about the words and significantly more about "sacrifice", then it could be indeed an eye opener in determining how much you love or others love you!

Now don't get me wrong, I am not saying you have to fall in love with those you lead! In fact, I am definitely not saying that! Nor am I saying that you have to have a "love" for them in the sense that you love your partner or mother! However, there has to be some degree of desire to make sacrifice for the person. That sacrifice will be time, that sacrifice will be to care about the things that they care about, and that sacrifice will be to carry maybe some of the burdens that they struggle with. Paid or unpaid, I think anyway, a leader must genuinely want to be sacrificial in their approach to the engagement and indeed as much as humanly possible, be selfless in the process.

- **The Push, Prod and Protect of leadership**

    Push: Push people, as they have great potential. Sometimes people need a gentle push to achieve great things, sometimes they need a big push and other times they need to be rammed like a wrecking ball!

    Prod: As I sat one day feeling a bit vulnerable to the constant barrage of unrealistic expectations of my boss and being metaphorically slapped for not meeting them, my PA gave me the explanation. "He's just prodding you Phil, he is just trying to see how you react, test you and get the best out of you." Sometimes as a leader we need to prod even though it can be painful and annoying!

    Protect: The leader is there to protect people in terms of their careers, their livelihoods, their development, and even their emotional and mental wellbeing. A leader must have a true sense of being the protector of those they guide.

BUILD UP YOUR WISDOM, KNOWLEDGE AND DISCERNMENT (WKD)

My "Start to Lead" book talked about the importance of leaders needing wisdom, knowledge and discernment (WKD). By the way I love the "WKD" acronym (not my idea, but it was a friend and great business guy called Mogue who came up with it as we were deliberating about the importance of wisdom, knowledge and discernment in leadership over a steak one evening). Without WKD, you can lead nothing and you will make a train wreck out of your mentoring sessions. Leaders deal with everything with a spirit of wisdom. Wisdom comes from knowledge and experience grounded in a desire to always do the right things. Wise heads can be on young shoulders, and foolish heads have been on many old shoulders - so age has nothing to do with it. Only wise people can be great mentors or leaders. A man or woman, who is known to be wise is a great and powerful influence in any environment. This is because they bring wisdom to complex challenges, they bring wisdom to conflict and they bring wisdom to taking the organisation forward. Wisdom leads to wise decisions and lack of wisdom leads to foolish decisions. Winston Churchill once said: "Character is the habit of making right decisions."

Discernment is also important and typically only comes with knowledge and experience. Discernment is the ability to tell truth from error. And in a world, that has a great deal of error and untruth in it, it is necessary to have the ability to discern in every situation and perceive where the truth lies.

START TO DO *SOME* INNOVATION

It would be crazy not to dedicate a specific section to the subject of innovation. It would be crazy because in times of crisis typically, there are significant changes in the economy, in society, and in your market that make innovation necessary in order to adapt to these changes and sustain your business. An easy example of innovation, at the time of writing during the Covid-19 crisis of 2020, is the complete shutdown of the hospitality industry that necessitated restaurants to innovate and move rapidly from a "sit-in" restaurant business model to a "take-away" or "home-delivery" business model. The only option in this example was for the restaurant to innovate or their sales would be zero – simple as that. Another example, would be a manufacturing business to retool and innovate in order to become a supplier of PPE equipment to the health service during a global pandemic. The restaurant innovation is keeping the same staff (albeit perhaps in a reduced number), the same product offering (again perhaps in a more limited range) but innovating in how it delivers to the customer and the focus needs to be in developing your logistical capacity to facilitate home delivery, developing online ordering and marketing your service now primarily through digital platforms. The manufacturing business has to innovate arguably in a more substantive way, in that different skill sets may be required, new products need developed, new machinery is required, new processes need developed, and the customer profile will also have changed.

SO, WHAT IS INNOVATION?

Innovation is doing things differently. It is doing things differently not for the sake of just being different, but to ensure the long-term profitable sustainability of your business. Innovation is of course the development of new products and services, but you can also innovate in a multitude of ways in your organisation that ensures the long-term profitable sustainability of your business. Innovation can be making technology changes in your internal administrative processes in order to achieve cost savings. Innovation can be changing your marketing tactics and strategy in order to increase sales. Innovation can be changing your operations and logistics in order to maximise efficiency and effectiveness. Sometimes innovation is a natural evolution of a mature business that is constantly adapting to changes in consumer behaviours, legislative changes and technology etc and other times innovation can be forced as the only alternative to survive. At the time of writing in the Covid-19 crisis of 2020, no matter where we were in terms of our past innovation credentials, at the time, we were all forced to think of ways of doing things differently.

HOW DO WE DO INNOVATION?

It's very easy to say "let's innovate," but how does that actually happen? As a leader or business owner, you may be thinking that you need to do things differently to survive and thrive, but what are the stages to making that happen?. Ok, here are the stages of making innovation happen in the organisation:

- **Recognise that innovation is necessary:** Everything starts with recognition! At this stage it is important to really believe that things have to change and things have to be done differently. And that comes from recognising that the environment that you operate in has changed significantly, and that presents a real and present danger to the short term, medium and perhaps long-term profitability and sustainability of your business.

- **Recognise that continuous innovation is about creating a culture:** My "Start to Lead" book gives some space to discuss innovation and in particular creating a culture that encourages innovation through, for example, giving people permission to think and reflect, come up with new ideas without fear of failure, training to innovate, mentoring to encourage innovation within the goals of the organisation and also encouraging it through the performance management systems etc.

- **Recognise that innovation can also be done quickly:** There are probably a number of innovations that your organisation has explored in the past but never activated for a number of reasons such as fear, cost, the challenges of implementing change and all those barriers that make us just put that innovation initiative on the shelf for another day. Well, during a crisis, those innovations can be taken off the shelf and potentially quickly implemented. It may be the implementation of technology that was in the past considered an optional luxury, but now it is a necessity to keep the business functioning profitably.

- **Target the areas in the business that need it:** This may seem an obvious point - innovate where innovation is necessary! However, we need to be focused. Therefore, make a list of what areas need innovation in order to adapt to the changes that are happening in your world. Part or all of your customer base may be decimated so the need will be to innovate in new products and services to a new market (like the PPE manufacturer already mentioned). There may be a need to cut costs across the board by 20% and that may mean introducing new processes and new technologies to allow a number of staff redundancies. Make a list and set the goals that you want to achieve and how you are going to do it with each area of the business that needs innovation.

- **Goals, ownership and accountability:** Innovation is a big thing in many ways and it needs to be treated as such. Therefore, for each area that you have identified that requires innovation, set goals that you want to achieve (cost saving, efficiency, enhanced service etc) and make sure someone has ownership of that innovation so they can be challenged and held to account. Goals, ownership, accountability and challenge function all need to be in the innovation journey.

- **Encourage company-wide innovation:** Say to everyone, there is a bonus for coming up with new ideas that save money! Simple as that. And facilitate this process by bringing teams together and allowing a spirit of brutal honesty by saying "ok, talk to me about things that you do that could be done better or more efficiently." You, as a leader, may have been a barrier to change or the staff could have been a barrier to change or others could have been a barrier to change – it doesn't matter – the key thing is that now is the time for openness and honesty among everyone, on ways things could be done better. This will actually be a motivating experience because many staff members can be burdened and become wearisome working with inefficient outdated processes that the staff member knows could be done much more efficiently. Now is the time to release all those innovations and changes that are just sitting there ready to activate.

- **Get the advisory board to encourage innovation:** A good board should be coming up with new ideas and bringing innovations to the table because of each board member's different skill set, experience and knowledge. The accountant, for example, may be able to advise on ways of operating the finance function more effectively through technology, or the chair could maybe advise on how to move into a different market. However, the main function of the advisory board and indeed the business advisor (if you bring one in) is to encourage innovation, challenge the leadership to innovate, and also hold everyone to account on making sure that innovation happens in the areas identified in order to achieve the goals that have been agreed.

START TO DO *MORE* MARKETING

Marketing is essentially "opening" and sales is "closing". Marketing is opening up opportunities, opening the market, opening doors, opening awareness, opening demand, opening up basically everything! Marketing is the art of opening and selling is the art of closing. Sales is closing the deal, taking the order and making money from all the investment in product, marketing and people that it took for you to get to the sale.

When reflecting on your marketing function in the business, you are essentially reflecting on your effectiveness in "opening" and your effectiveness in "closing." Obviously, marketing is a big subject and highly specialised with rapidly changing marketing platforms and changing ways that we engage with customers - so I am just going to set out some thoughts that any business should consider when the subject of "marketing" comes up during a crisis. And in true marketing speak all the points will start with the letter, you guessed it, "P"!!!

- **Plan**

  The first thing to consider – do you have a marketing plan?

  Marketing can be conducted in a very ad hoc, emotive, knee jerk, sometimes ego centric way at times in a business (particularly in a small business). Budget constraints can impact marketing activity and cause the brakes to be applied for months and then marketing can be reignited again when there is a bit of extra cash or perhaps sheer panic due to sales dipping, or just as a result of an over-enthusiastic owner who has just noticed a great marketing campaign that they would like to replicate!

  In addition, there can also exist a general anti-marketing sentiment amongst the directors or partners of a business. There can be a widely held view that delivery (operations) and support to delivery (administration) are the main functions that need activity, energy, resources and money and therefore, marketing inevitably becomes a bit of an afterthought with the left-over crumbs of budget and time.

  Therefore, to cut through all of this, there needs to be an agreed marketing plan. A "marketing plan" can sometimes appear to others as a bit academic and an unnecessary waste of time. I understand this sentiment, so it is important to put together a document that is not too heavy but sets out the marketing activities, resources, budgets and implementation for the next 6-12 months during the

crisis. The plan needs to state what "good" looks like, in other words, what the business wants to achieve in terms of sales, profit, market share, customer retention. There then needs to be a series of activities (PR, advertising, social media, etc) properly costed with timelines for implementation. Everything should be measured in terms of impact and linked to overall goals that have been set for the organisation.

- People

    Who owns marketing in the organisation? Someone needs to own it, be accountable for carrying it out successfully and be living and breathing it. It may lie with the owner in a small business or with a team, but someone in the organisation needs to be ultimately responsible for the marketing function.

    Your business needs to ensure that there are the human resources in place to deliver on the marketing plan. And not only are there people in place, but also that they have the skills, ability, resources and key competencies to implement effectively. In addition, there needs to be a strong accountability and challenge function put in place to ensure that they deliver on individual and organisational marketing goals. Sometimes budgets may not permit, or it may not even be necessary, to have a full time marketing resource but it is important that those responsible for marketing have a plan, the resources to implement the plan and there is a strong accountability and challenge function to ensure the agreed plan is implemented effectively.

- Partners

  Make sure your business has great marketing partners. When it comes to the function of marketing, in my view, you don't have suppliers, you have partners. Partners are organisations that support your marketing activity such as design companies, PR agencies, SEO specialists, printing firms, and digital marketing consultants etc. These partners should be trusted, well regarded, exceptional organisations that "get" your business and provide a consistency, continuity and quality that ensures a powerful marketing function that delivers exceptional results.

  Review the marketing "partners" in the organisation to ensure they meet the highest standards. Challenge the "supplier" mentality and encourage a "partnership" approach that looks at building enduring long-term relationships with quality organisations. You may want to create a marketing forum that brings marketing support partners together every quarter for an hour and a half to review activity (this should be free as they get business from you and potentially more business as a result of the forum!). This forum will ensure there is consistency right across the marketing partners in relation to the company's marketing activity, and the forum will also facilitate good co-ordination, strategic thinking, new ideas and creativity to ensure the marketing activity is innovative, creative and adaptable to a rapidly changing business environment.

- Processes

  Regardless of the size of the company, there should be good marketing systems and processes embedded in the organisation. The marketing partners should be in place, and there should be a forum every quarter to ensure that the marketing activity is consistent, co-ordinated and effective. In addition, as much as possible, marketing activities should be automated to ensure that marketing is an ongoing consistent process in the organisation. There should be agreed marketing reports delivered on a regular basis, targets in relation to social media activity, meetings and forums that should be scheduled to happen etc.

- Position strongly in the digital space

    Dominating the digital space means that you are visible to your market when they are on the internet or social media platforms. And you should aim to be ahead of your competitors in this space.

    Pay for an independent review of your digital marketing activity. No matter how good you think you are in the digital space, invest in a digital marketing review with a reputable digital marketing company. Typically, go with an independent digital marketing consultant who will not necessarily be steering you into spending a fortune with them on the "recommendations" section. The review will give you an independent assessment of your full digital presence on social media and the internet and give recommendations for going forward. Don't let the review sit on the shelves. Implement the recommendations of the review and spend the money.

START TO GET *HOLD* OF THE FINANCIALS

- **Get on top of the key numbers**

    Business growth is about understanding the numbers and in my view it is too late to see those key numbers a few months after your financial year-end. If you have been making losses or too much cash has been going out of the business, by the time you sit down with your accountant a year down the line to review the numbers, a lot of damage may have already been done. It's like neglecting changing your brake pads on your car... by the time you have to sort the problem out, the pads have worn down and metal hits metal and then there is a lot more damage and cost that could have been avoided (I give the example from personal experience and still haven't learnt, much to my business partner James' despair!). Every business needs to ensure they are on top of the key numbers - monthly, weekly, even daily! A great friend and mentor of James and I advised us to do management accounts and we will be eternally grateful to Will for this timely advice that served us well for many years. I would suggest you always ensure that you get an accountant internally or externally to provide them.

Get the accountant or financial controller to provide management accounts, at least quarterly so you know what the financial picture is throughout the financial year rather than six months after the end of it! As well as having management accounts prepared every month or quarter, make sure you can understand them or get your accountant to explain them. I, for one, need them explained to me. The accountant needs to tell you if there are any danger signs, positive or negative trends in your business, if your costs need to be trimmed or prices need to rise. The accountant needs to have a 'state of the nation' discussion every quarter for an hour, just so they have an intimate and full understanding of the financial workings of your business. If this isn't happening, whether you are watching the bank online every day or monitoring your sales figures, you don't know the full picture and you could be running into trouble. If your accountant is not lightening responsive to your needs – dump them! No matter how long you have known them, or how friendly they are with your uncle Benny or how awkward you feel confronting them – if they are not "with you" on this journey of recovery, then dump them and go with the new generation of work smart/tech accountants who will support your needs highly effectively.

- Price for profit

    Don't price to win, don't price to build market share and don't price to beat competition… you need to price to make profit. I know all the arguments with this and I know all the other considerations and I on many occasions have 'dropped them', but at the end of the day, if you don't price for profit, your business will go bust and it is as simple as that. As you look around the business world, many businesses are having to raise prices. Why? I suspect because their accountants or bank managers are telling them to - they are not *asking* them to raise prices, they are *telling* them! Many businesses have adopted a pile it high and sell it cheap strategy to build their business and that is fine. There are budget business models out there that work, but they are well thought through and without a doubt, with the successful ones, the margins are there. The businesses have just been clever in hiding them but the profitability is there. However, those exceptions aside, we have to price for profit and make sure we have a good margin that ensures that our business can cover overheads, make profit and build cash. Any business that wants to be around in the long term needs to adopt this strategy.

- **Get a grip on credit control**

  You can be saving your pennies, keeping on top of the numbers, and pricing for profit but losing grip on your credit control will kill your business. Whoever does it, be it you or a staff member, credit control needs to be a regular process within the organisation. You need to ensure that customers are paying within their terms and if they are not, you need to keep the pressure on. Simple tips for this would be;

✓ Get cash on delivery as much as possible
✓ Don't delay, call the customer the day after late payment

- ✓ Be persistent in getting what is due to you
- ✓ Have good T's & C's to give you 'options' if payment is delayed
- ✓ And get paid by DD if you can!

- **The 5% trick – increase profits by 45% (you will love this)**

    My former MD taught me this. With the market contracting and less pie to go around you can actually increase your profits by 45% by just moving costs and sales by 5%!! Very clever. Here's how to do it.

    The 5% trick is how you can increase profit by 45% without having to grow business sales by 45% (which may be impossible in a crisis). Say for example your sales are £100,000 and your overhead is £80,000 and your profit is therefore £20,000 and you want to grow profit by 45%. Sounds crazy but this can be done! To grow profit by 45% typically we will grow sales to do this and overheads largely follow too.

    Sales: £145,000
    Overhead: £116,000
    Profit: £29,000

    However, there is no way sales are growing by 45% during this crisis! Therefore, again let's say for example your sales are £100,000 and your overhead is £80,000 and your profit is therefore £20,000.

    Sales: £100,000
    Overhead: £80,000
    Profit: £20,000

This time if you reduce the £80,000 overhead by just 5% across the board and sales stay the same at £100,000, overhead reduces to £76,000 and profit is now £24,000. The profit has actually achieved straight away a 20% growth!

Sales: £100,000
Overhead: £76,000 (5% reduction)
Profit: £24,000 (20% growth)

If you then, in addition to the 5% reduction in costs, do a very small 5% increase in prices, then sales grow to £105,000, overhead is still at £76,000 but profit is now £29,000! And this is 45% growth in profit!

Sales: £105,000
Overhead: £76,000
Profit: £29,000 (45% Growth)

So for now, do the 5% trick and see the magic unfold!

SECTION TWO
MENTORING & PUBLIC SPEAKING

START TO...
MENTOR
OTHERS

INTRODUCTION

What?! Start giving advice? Why in the world would I want to start going around "mentoring people" when my business is in meltdown? I understand the reaction and I understand the sentiment. However, one of the phrases that has come up time and time again during the current crisis that I am writing this book in, is that "we are all in this together." And if we are all in this together, we need to help one another. You need to help me and I need to help you – we all need to help one another. And in that spirit of helping one another, then the business leader can take the opportunity to mentor others and help them on their journey of recovery.

A good mentor is someone who looks at a person and determines in their heart and mind that they, at some level, care about that person, and because they care about them, they want to help them on their personal journey. That help may be for a short time, a period of months or it could be a long enduring mentor – mentee relationship.

In life you should have at least a mentor and a protégé - Someone to give advice to and someone to take advice from (someone said this but I can't recall who!)

The nature of the mentoring will vary. The following are some of the types of mentoring I have observed, experienced and carried out myself personally:

Technical mentoring. The mentor has expertise in a particular area and they advise, inform, explain and educate the mentee in a particular subject matter. The mentor's knowledge and understanding and insights far exceed the mentee's capability in this subject matter and so the dynamic is one of educating. For example, this could be seen with a finance director mentoring a young accountant who has just joined the firm.

Developmental mentoring. The mentor seeks to develop the person in certain "soft" areas that are important to the mentee. These areas may be confidence, communication skills, interpersonal skills, management style, and leadership etc. The mentor would be someone who is considered "exceptional" in the particular areas that are focused on in this mentor-mentee relationship.

Friendly mentoring: The mentor and mentee are friends, the relationship is informal, and the mentor is unlikely to be paid. There is mutual respect and the mentor typically will encourage, advise, and help the mentee with whatever particular matters the mentee may be facing at that time. There are friendly encouragements, sometimes challenging tones and a little bit of accountability but overall, it's two buddies sharing the journey and, in many ways, benefitting equally from one another.

Formal mentoring: This is probably paid work and the dynamic is formal and structured. There will be regular meetings with set times and parameters will be set in terms of the duration of the meeting and its content.

This type of formal mentoring is where objectives are set, goals are identified, plans of action are put in place and a strong accountability and challenge function is in the mentor-mentee relationship.

Strategic mentoring: This will happen typically in an organisation that is going through particular significant change where you need gravitas and wealth of experience from the mentor who has "been there and done it" a million times and understands all the wrinkles, all the issues and all the potential pitfalls. The mentor in this relationship is a heavyweight through and through! Bring this type of mentor into your world if you are going to buy a business, expand globally, take on a new acquisition or plan to grow the business double digit for the next five years. My business partner and I brought in a guy called Will for this task and indeed he was a serious heavyweight and experienced businessman.

Advisory mentoring: This is where you meet with someone and they hit you with issues and matters that need to be addressed in their life or their business. As a mentor, you are good at taking a "30,000 ft look at things", you are quick to grasp the issues and what needs to be done and you offer solutions to the problems that they are facing.

Job specific mentoring: This mentoring will be carried out by someone who has already fulfilled the role of the mentee. In other words, a senior pastor or retired pastor mentoring a young trainee pastor just entering into ministry. The mentor is guiding, encouraging, advising (both formally and informally) the mentee over a period of time until the mentee is essentially no longer needing that level of input from the mentor.

When you mentor someone, it is likely that you will be a mix of at least two of these roles. The conversation may include some developmental advice, a bit of job specific mentoring and maybe at some stage, straightforward technical mentoring on how to actually "do" something.

WHAT MENTORING ROLE TO ADOPT?

It's an obvious point but you can adopt any of these mentoring roles, and do it well as long as you fit the bill! In other words, only do job specific mentoring if you have had at least five years' experience in that particular job or only be a strategic mentor if you have considerable experience and knowledge in business growth and development. Don't start mentoring someone on finance or human resources unless you are highly knowledgeable and proven in those particular fields. This should be all fairly obvious but it amazes me how so many people set themselves up as "mentors" with neither the knowledge or experience and/or credentials to fulfil the role in a way that will help the mentee. In fact, the wrong mentor relationship can have a significant negative impact on the mentee. Therefore, it is really important to choose your mentees carefully. Only engage in a mentoring relationship with someone that you can add real value to, that you can genuinely help and, importantly, someone that you genuinely care about.

IDENTIFYING A MENTEE?

I suggest that identifying people to mentor is something that should happen quite naturally and organically. A person will come into your world or will at least be on your radar and should be someone who, from the previous paragraph:

"looks at a person and determines in their heart and mind that they, at some level, care about that person, and because they care about them, they want to help them on their individual journey."

Sometimes, of course, you will be approached and asked directly. A lady who attended one of my seminars rang me up and just asked me directly if I could be her mentor. I didn't know her but I knew that I could fulfil some advisory and developmental mentoring with her. We agreed on a fee, met once a month and after six months of the engagement, the objectives of the engagement were achieved.

Whoever you decide to mentor, make sure that you really can add value to them and/or their organisation. You may have to turn away from agreeing to do some mentoring simply because you don't feel you can add value to that relationship even though you would, at one level, love to do it. I recently turned down a four day a month assignment at a substantial daily rate simply because I didn't feel I could fulfil the unique set of expectations and requirements of that particular role. That wasn't an easy decision!

When mentoring someone, you need to get below the surface, get beyond the bravado, move away from the niceties, and the small talk and try to get a deeper understanding of the mentee standing before you. Like me, many will not let you in too deep but at least go on a journey to know the real person a bit more every time you meet. And you may know more about them by what they directly tell you but you also will get to know them at a deeper level by what they don't say and what you carefully observe.

MENTORING IS ESSENTIALLY ABOUT FINDING SOLUTIONS TO PROBLEMS

My early mentor Trevor said to me in my first mentoring session with him, "with every problem that you come to me with – I want you to have three solutions." I never forgot this statement. This one statement made it clear to me what mentoring was essentially about. From Trevor's statement, mentoring was about the following:

- **Identifying issues/problems:** The mentee is to identify issues and problems that are significant enough to need addressing and requiring of a solution going forward.

- **Personal ownership.** The mentee needs to have ownership of the issues that need to be addressed (they aren't enforced or set by the mentor). The dynamic of the relationship is that it is essentially all about the mentee.

- **Solutions orientated:** The mentor-mentee relationship is not just about "chewing the fat" as they say. It is about actually coming up with good solutions to short, medium or long-term issues and problems.

- **Exploratory:** Finding the right solutions to the issues identified by the mentee is through exploring their own solutions with the mentor. The mentor will stress test the solutions, challenge them, perhaps refine them, and even dismiss them if they are unworkable (some solutions offered can actually be rubbish and it's ok to tell the mentee that!).

- **The mentee is proactive:** Trevor made it clear that this relationship was mentee driven by stating – "every problem that you come to me with". In other words, the mentee is to use their initiative to come to the mentor, the mentee is to be essentially driving the relationship, showing ownership and a desire to move forward in the areas identified.

- **The mentor is the first among equals:** The mentor has got to be seen as the senior. It isn't really a relationship of equals. The mentor is the senior hand and the more authoritative figure. And it has to be this way because they are going to be challenging the mentee and holding them to account. At times, the mentor may want to push and prod a bit as well as protect the mentee and to do this he/she has to essentially be in charge.

THE MENTORING DYNAMIC

ENCOURAGE PLAIN SPEAKING

Often in relationships, we refrain from saying stuff in fear of offending the other person. We hold back in being direct and straight with the person, and that can sometimes be a good thing and other times a bad thing. I have to say my experience with CEO's and early career mentors was that the language they used was direct and colourful enough. One CEO told me that I had "(expletive) - dropped the ball", and another one told me that "a number of people in this organisation don't like you," and another said angrily "don't think that you run this business." They were all direct comments that jolted me. They had told me the hard truth and, if I wanted to be anywhere near the finished article as a business person, I needed to address those hard truths or at least be aware of them. The comment about thinking I owned the business was more a driver to actually "own" a business and a few years later I set up ShredBank with my business partner and friend James!

When mentoring someone, make sure you don't hold back. The mentee needs to know all the encouraging and positive stuff but they also need to hear the more difficult truths. And sometimes they also need to hear those difficult truths clearly, directly and unambiguously (though try to refrain from any expletives!).

FOCUS ON ONE OR TWO ISSUES MAXIMUM

Each mentoring session should be about tackling one, or at most, two issues. This can be flexible, as the journey of dealing with one issue may raise a much bigger issue that needs to be focused on instead. Many years ago, a mentoring session that I had with a guy about sales performance led to a discussion about his personal life that meant the sales performance discussion was ditched and the rest of the session and, indeed future sessions were around his personal life. With this guy, the mentoring ensured that his personal life was sorted out and subsequently the sales performance naturally sorted itself out!

FOCUS ON THE RIGHT ISSUES

Following on from the point above, you can be clocking up a lot of time mentoring an individual discussing the wrong issue. They may want to discuss a particular issue, you may want to accommodate them in discussing that issue, but as the conversation progresses, you may discern that this is the wrong topic of conversation. The right issue may well be the elephant in the room, or the overarching issue that affects all other issues, or simply an issue the mentee just doesn't want to confront, but nevertheless it must be discussed. Find the right issues and focus on them.

PARTNERSHIP APPROACH

Consider the mentor-mentee relationship as a partnership. In many ways my definition of leadership (seen in my previous book – "Start to Lead") can apply to some degree to the mentor – mentee relationship. My definition of leadership is

"Creating an environment that enables goals to be achieved."

You are both in that relationship to achieve goals and in order to achieve those goals you need to work together to create an environment that enables that to happen. The environment may be relating to organisational changes that need to be made, people that need to be developed or cultures that need changed. Or the environment may be internal, and it is all about the mentee and therefore, the personal changes that they need to address, may well be what the mentoring focus needs to be on.

GOAL ORIENTATED

Following on from the previous point, the relationship must be goal orientated. Goals must be agreed and set. The goals don't need to be set in a formulaic way or with flip charts (though they could be if you wish). In my view, goals are better set naturally and organically throughout the conversations. And as you explore issues and as you get to the "right issues", then goals should naturally flow out of that conversation. And yes, you can write them down but try to aim for, and this will sound corny, writing the goals on the heart rather than on a tablet or sheet of paper. You don't want to have too many goals so they shouldn't be too hard to remember!

ALLOW THEM TO SPEAK

Mentors can be know-it-alls who like the sound of their own voice. They can just be full of answers, solutions and insights and they really see the mentee's role as listening and actioning anything the mentor dishes out. I am not innocent here as I have often veered into the "stay quiet and listen to me" mode. However, people can often react to this type of approach emotionally and clam up on you. And that emotional response will lead them to becoming defensive, possibly confrontational and essentially the mentor-mentee relationship could become broken. The mentor needs to ask questions that brings the mentee to the heart of the issue and then explore solutions after that. I don't want to be too prescriptive here about the types of questions that you would ask, because if I do, the danger is that a mentor reading this will engage with the mentee in a very scripted, "mentorish" (my word) style which is just totally off-putting for the mentee and will not be conducive to the relationship building/partnership approach that you are aiming for.

DON'T ALLOW THEM TO SPEAK

However, sometimes people actually do need to just "stay quiet and listen" as the mentor tells them how it is and what they need to do. Some professional coaches will be shocked by this point that I am making. Undoubtedly there is a time to allow the mentee to explore within themselves and come up with a solution and answer that lies within, but other times they need to be eye-balled and told what needs doing! We live in a world of so many shades of grey, so many opinions and counter views that most people are just plain confused as to what to do. And in my opinion, there are times when people just need answers and they need it delivered in black and white, no ambiguity and with clarity and conviction that provides a roadmap going forward.

PAY CLOSE ATTENTION TO THE SIGNS

A mentor needs to pay close attention to the person that they are mentoring. Close attention to their stress levels, their emotional state, perhaps personal issues that are impacting on their life. You need to pay close attention because you should care about that person and not just care that they achieve goals, but you care about them in every sense of the word. And part of caring about them is caring about their entire wellbeing. Someone's emotional or mental state and/or the personal issues that they are dealing with, for many people, are a very personal thing and indeed they may not want to be shared. You can observe them carefully and gently seek to help in any areas that are very obvious but you always have to tread carefully in this issue. Addressing emotional or personal issues has got to be *permission based* and you have got to build trust, respect and a depth in the relationship for these discussions to happen. However, keep the entirety of their wellbeing in mind and watch for the signs, and then, at the bare minimum, say enough so that they will know that they can talk to you and you will always be a listening ear and an understanding heart.

SECTION TWO
MENTORING & PUBLIC SPEAKING

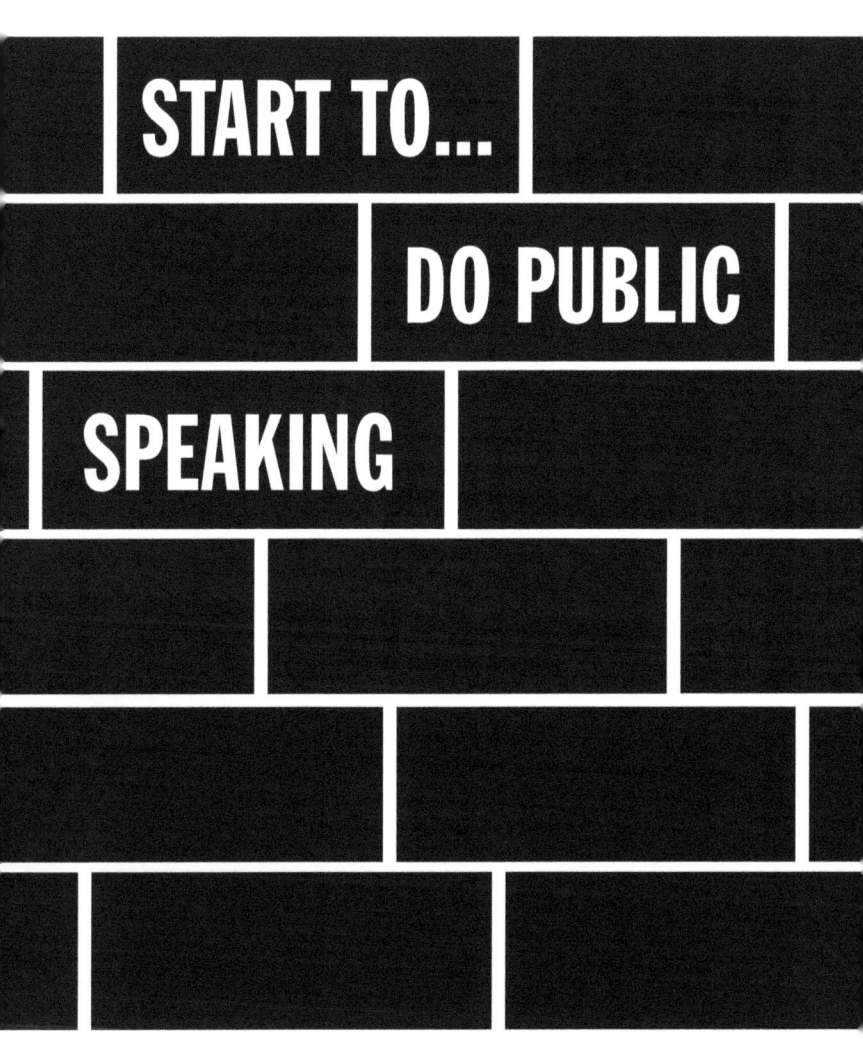

INTRODUCTION

Again, you may say, "why in the world would I want to share my story and take to the stage and do public speaking?" Well, first of all, it is free publicity – lecturing at university, colleges, enterprise agencies, events etc is a great way to raise your company's profile. Secondly, all leaders need to master the art of the narrative, in other words, storytelling. Essentially, selling is storytelling, and marketing is storytelling in that, when you are selling or marketing, you are telling a story about your business and the products and services it sells and how they change the world. You are telling a story and you need to get better at storytelling in order to get better at selling and marketing your business. And for me, the best way to learn that, is through public speaking.

LET ME TELL YOU MY STORY ON THE PUBLIC SPEAKING THING

"Your son doesn't say anything, he's very quiet!" my P2 teacher said to my mum as I was sitting eating a ½ pence chew rather awkwardly and counting the seconds to get the heck out of there. It was another parent meeting at the school to complain about my overall mediocrity and lack of engagement in class. Quiet, anti-social and a bit odd, seemed to be how I was described by most of the people around me when I was young (and I also seemed to puke milk up a lot because I drank it too quickly!). The notion that the anti-social milk-puker would be a guest lecturer, public speaker and preacher from my 20s onwards would have seemed laughable at the time! Probably still seems laughable to those who have known me from an early age!

My general shyness and timidity caused me to look at my shoes most of the time (and I'm told that I still do this), and being sociable meant for me just looking at other people's shoes! Academically I was also a disaster. That was until I learnt the art of doing exams and dissertations, which in this jurisdiction was thankfully, pretty much not to do with having a high level of intelligence. My Dad's early advice that *exams are all about technique* served me well over those early academic years! A learned exam technique and a photographic memory kept the grades in reasonable (ish) shape to get me across the line!

Anyway, for those reasons, public speaking was never on the agenda, until a couple of years into university, when I did a presentation as part of one of my modules. Most of my presentations leading up to this point were group presentations, messy stuck together acetate sheets (you have to be born in the 60s and 70s to know what an acetate sheet is), dummy cards and an awkward stuttering effort that is best forgotten. However, it was during my final year that public speaking seemed to lift up a gear or two for me. I can't remember what the presentation was about, but I just remember it was one of those moments that you never forget. It was something pivotal. As I took to the stage, I just seemed to get this confidence that was absent from me in most social circles. I remember as I started to speak that I had a sense of real ownership of the subject and a deep belief that what I had to say had value. I had no notes and bags of unexplained confidence which led to it being one of those "I can do this" moments. The presentation on that day proved to me that shyness was not necessarily a barrier to speaking publicly, and it shouldn't be for others either.

Within a few months of delivering my talk in university, I was working for a great company as part of my industrial placement year and had the privilege of hearing a memorable talk by a highly charismatic CEO of the company. The CEO inspired, he entertained, he informed and he delivered something really special that seemed to move people and motivate them in ways that I had never seen before. It was powerful and unforgettable. Since then, I have heard many talks from the great and good and most of them fell well short of the standard I witnessed that day in the conference room of Antrim Technology Park. However, it was listening to that guy, that made me realise the power of communication. In one talk, you had the power to do something really special, you had the power to lift up someone who felt low, to inspire people to make a difference, to motivate, instruct, and even encourage.

Shortly after the university talk, I was given an opportunity to preach in my local church. I was really nervous and after the talk I was told there were a few errors in what I said and I then was brought down to earth by a chat with an experienced preacher. Sometimes these early corrections, critiques and criticisms can kill confidence, but try and take them as constructive and useful. By the way, I didn't take the comments as constructive and useful but that's another story.

I then got a number of opportunities to speak in more informal gatherings and then things really kicked off, when I was asked to speak on tendering at a networking conference. I declined the offer initially as I felt that I couldn't speak authoritatively on the subject but, if they wanted me to speak on growing a business during a recession (which I happened to be doing at the time) then I would agree to do it. They agreed, I spoke for 20 minutes at the event, and the response was unexpectedly positive. From that point on, I have been asked to do about 20-30 talks a year. The rest as they say…

As well as public speaking, over the years, I have found great opportunities to mentor and advise others on their journey and I have been privileged to learn as much from them as I hope they have from me. Talking is really now all that I actually do! I do very little administration, thankfully my business partner and I have a fabulous team who are brilliant at it. I also do very little operations as we have equally amazing operatives to deliver on that side of the business. My business partner James handles expertly the operational and administrative leadership of the business. My day is spent just talking – selling, negotiating, marketing, mentoring, advising and, few times a month, lecturing and public speaking.

I learnt fairly early on in life, the power of words – the power of talking. Out of your mouth can come words that could discourage, deflate, and even destroy someone. Or you could utter words that could encourage, lift and give renewed life to someone. The tongue is a powerful force. If used well, the tongue can be a small member of the body used for a great purpose, but if used wrongly, even though it may be a small member of the body, it can cause great damage.

Why not share your story? You have built an enterprise, you have started it...grown it and are now leading it. What you have learnt from the experiences of that journey can now be told. It can be told publicly, it can be told one to one, it can be told by teaching, conversing, advising, mentoring or coaching. Whatever is in there - now is the time to let it out and to advise, encourage and inspire. Now is the time to share your story.

TO SPEAK OR NOT TO SPEAK THAT IS THE QUESTION

If there is an opportunity for you to do a public speaking event, then it is important to determine whether you should actually do it or not. As I mentioned earlier, I was asked several years ago to do a talk on "Tendering." I told the person organising the event that I would not be able to speak on that particular subject because, although I have done many tenders in my business life, I would not consider myself to be an expert in tendering, nor would I be comfortable speaking on the subject to an audience that may well ask a question that I couldn't answer, and therefore destroy my credibility in an instant.

Instead, I gave the person organising the event an alternative topic that I could credibly speak on. I told them I could speak on "Growing your business during a recession." I said that I was currently growing ShredBank, the business my business partner James and I started during the recession, and I could talk both knowledgeably and indeed experientially about the subject. Having lived and breathed business growth my entire career, I was confident that I could deliver a talk, engage people and field questions on this subject. After a brief discussion, they agreed to let me speak on business growth rather than tendering. I turned up at the event, did my 20 minutes talk and I have been doing similar talks ever since.

The point of the story is that, I would suggest, you should never speak on any subject that you have not either the highest of academic credentials and/or significant experience in. For me, and I expect for most people, the value of any presentation is not regurgitating or repackaging what "others" are saying, rather, it is telling the audience what "you" are saying which is based on *your* own personal experience, understanding and insights on the subject. Anyone can talk about what someone else said, and for me, this is of little value to the listener who has probably paid to go to the event. However, to hear the authoritative and experienced words of someone who has been there and done it and got the bruises and the trophies, is infinitely more valuable to the listener.

UNDERSTANDING THE BRIEF

Understanding the brief of *why* they want you to speak and what they want you to speak on, is obviously fundamental. The details of what you are going to say when you present - that is up to you. How you are going to present – that is also up to you. However, you need to know why they want you to speak. Are you there to inspire? Are you there to educate? Are you there to give highly technical information that needs deep explanation? Are you there to present data-rich facts? You need to understand why they want you to speak, what the event organiser's objectives are and what they want to achieve.

You also need to find out the composition of the audience. In other words, what do the audience want? Why are they turning up at the event? What are their expectations? When I am going to speak at an event, I will typically ask the organisers what is the makeup of the audience and what businesses they run? I will ask if they are established businesses with experienced business owners or are they new start-ups, with little or no staff, looking to get to the next stage in their business growth, or are they aspiring entrepreneurs, or is the audience a combination of all three types? I will want to know the audience, understand why I am there and what the expectations of the paymasters are – I suggest you do the same.

PUTTING YOUR PRESENTATION TOGETHER

Having understood the brief and got it clear in your mind – maybe even documented it on paper - and having thought and reflected over the subject, now is the time to start putting pen to paper and bringing the presentation together. I am not going to get too technical here and give you an ABC presentation outline. The reason for that is that when someone has been formally trained on how to present or how to preach, you typically will hear an ABC presentation outline in their talk! That is grim and everyone sees through it. However, I would suggest that the presentation is put together on a number of key principles that I want to share with you:

- **Originality**

    Following on from the previous paragraph, make sure your presentation is about *your* insights, *your* thoughts and *your* reflections. This requires you to dig deep and reflect on your experiences, bring to mind situations that you can relay to the audience, and to give rich nuggets of information that are actually going to help them and to add value to their lives in one way or another. If it is a rip off, or part rip off of other people's work, then why should anyone listen to you or pay for you to be there? They might as well search for it on the internet and be done with it!

- **Purpose**

    It has to be a presentation that has purpose. It has to be about taking people on a journey with a beginning, a mid-way and an end destination. There has to be a point to what you are saying, a purpose to your presentation. The point of the talk may be to have the audience's hair stand up on the back of their neck, it may be to make them roll about laughing, it may be to inspire them, it may be to educate them about stuff they know they don't know, or really blow them away by telling them something they don't know they don't know! Whatever you do, make sure you have a purpose to your talk!

- **Content**

    The content has got to be really good. It has to be exceptional. Why? Well, think of the content delivered from a sermon, a seminar, or any talk that people gather around and listen to. The people who come to listen to you are not paying for or setting time aside for the purpose of hearing some average message. They are not there to hear stuff they know or stuff they could know if they downloaded it off the internet. They are wanting to hear your unique take on something - the content may not be technically unique, in that it may be the basics of marketing but how you package it, explain it, illustrate it and apply it should come with a freshness that engages the listener. It should be delivered in a way that will enhance understanding, that is actionable and that has application for them!!

- **Simplicity**

  Most people, and I emphasise most people, want things simple. The subject could be complex but your job is to bring simplicity. The presentation has to be simple not just in the language that you use and the simplicity of explanation, but also simple in the flow of the presentation, how it is structured, and the level of detail. Simplicity is so important to ensure people stay engaged, their brain continues to take it all in, and they see clearly the value that the talk brings to them.

- **Value**

  With every point you make in your talk you need to ask what value this will bring to others. With a business talk, for example, the value may be techniques that you share with them to ensure a better recruitment process that delivers better quality employees and a higher employee retention rate. Or it could be specific, actionable strategies that ensure that their organisation will increase its profile in the market and therefore generate more sales. Everything that you say has got to be of great value to the audience.

- **Application**

  Talk about original stuff in a way that is simple and adds value to people but also make sure you explain how people can make application of that information in their own lives. You have given the insights and reflection, now people need to know what to do with that! A pastor said to me once that people will make the applications for themselves. I would be sceptical about that. At the very least, you must recognise that the potential exists for people not to make the applications for themselves! It will therefore do no harm, and indeed add significantly to your presentation, if you tell people what they now must "do." Your talk needs to hit home to the audience how all of this good stuff that you are spouting about looks like for them on a Monday morning when they go into work. The audience needs the road map on how all these great insights that you are sharing are lived out and worked out in their lives and their businesses.

PREPARING YOUR PRESENTATION

- Take notes

    Have notes for your talk. I repeat – have notes for your talk! I have a photographic memory and I never use notes in business talks but I do have them in sermons that I preach. Largely because of the gravity of handling God's Word but also, though secondary in importance, I have a very vivid memory of a man speaking one evening without notes and forgetting the final third of his message. That train wreck I have no intention of repeating, so the notes stay for sermons (I'll say more about this in the next paragraph). However, for those who don't have a photographic memory, make sure you have the notes as a back-up, as a guide, and as an invisible support. Don't become glued to the notes and overly dependent on them. If you have to excessively hold the notes, look at them and read them, I would suggest don't bother speaking.

    As I said, I remember a guy speaking publicly without notes. He had been given an official title and had, I suspect, felt that he had to impress with delivering a talk without notes (before I go any further, never *try* to impress – it never works). Anyway, his points were "go low", "go slow" and ...well there wasn't a third point - not for the teeth clenching audience anyway - because he completely forgot the third point. He didn't know what to say and ended up having to close mid-way through his talk. Total disaster! Maybe others forgot about that but I didn't. I never forgot the fact that he had forgotten the third point. Never be in a position where you forget the third point, or any point! If you have any possibility that you might take a mind blank...always have notes that will carry you through! It is an unforgettable train wreck if you have to sit down gingerly because you have forgotten a third of the presentation.

- **Present to the wall... over and over again until you own it**

Present to the wall over and over again until you own it. Do the full talk as if it was the real thing with the audience. Use notes at the start but then as you repeat the presentation over and over again, use the notes less and less. Have a pen in your hand as you may add in points when you are rehearsing, so be ready to scribble extra stuff.

- **Own it**

Own the talk like it is a part of you. It can't be something detached from you as a separate talk that is out there somewhere. Own it intellectually, emotionally and mentally. You can only deliver it with passion and authenticity if you own it. Believe in it and I mean really believe in it, because you will deliver it with conviction. A talk with conviction is powerful for the listener and potentially life changing.

- **Technology**

    I have seen death by Powerpoint and I have seen it as a great support to an exceptional presentation - and I suspect you have seen this too. I have also seen speakers talk without any visuals at all and it can be exceptional, mediocre or dire. I am not going to focus too much on this point but rather give you the principle. Use visuals if you feel that they are relevant and necessary. If they are not, then leave it. Don't do it because you assume that it is the standard format that everyone wants and expects. It is indeed the standard format that many speakers use but it definitely is not always the format that people need.

- **Flip charts**

    Confession – I am a fan of flip charts! I love the flexibility and interactivity of them. Give me a few pens of different colours, preferably blue, red and black and a flip chart (preferably one that allows you to flip and not those awkward ones!) and I am a happy man! A couple of flip charts can be really interesting and it can really enhance the visual display of the presentation and the interactivity. However, having said that, one of my pet hates is when the speaker takes the sheets of the presentation and one by one sticks them up on the wall! Hate that...really hate that.

DAY OF THE PRESENTATION

- **Eat before you go**

  Get some food into you as you don't know what the event organisers are serving up! It may be lovely or rotten! Also, you may be nervous and do not feel like eating just before you speak. Therefore, before you leave the house make sure you are fed and watered with food and drink that you want and like, rather than what someone else is serving you. Also, eating and drinking minutes before a talk can cause all sorts of problems to some people from bloating to well, you know the stuff I mean! Therefore, before your talk, don't walk about with a bacon bap stuffed in your face with the tomato sauce sloutering (colloquialism) down your shirt or dress! Forget that! Eat before you leave the house!

- **Go over the talk one last time**

  Go over the presentation to get it fresh again in your heart and mind. Doing the talk one last time builds up your confidence, and ensures that you minimise the possibility of forgetting lines or losing your flow during a presentation.

- **Timekeeping**

    Make sure you know how to get to the location that you are going to be speaking at and arrive about 45 minutes before the event begins (not 45 minutes before you are going to speak). This gives you time to speak to event organisers, get comfortable with your surroundings, and of course deal with any technical issues regarding your presentation if required. You need a bit of time to get all of that practical and personable stuff sorted out.

DELIVERING THE PRESENTATION

As you take to the stage, there are a number of things I want to suggest you do at this point.

- **No grand entrances**

  One guy that I had asked to speak at an event that I was organising, wanted to make a grand entrance by walking from the back of the room through the middle of the audience. I think this is a bit over the top and may not necessarily cut any ice with the audience. I would just avoid grand entrances. On another occasion, in a church, the speaker got up very quickly while the music group was still on stage preparing to come off stage. He swaggered up to the podium with very misplaced confidence as if he owned the place and he started to shout in a broad accent with, I assume, the intention of conveying that he was some sort of seasoned maverick speaker who could conduct himself and behave in whatever way he wanted. Wrong move on his part, I don't believe that an audience responds well to this type of approach.

- **The opening**

    Intros and pleasantries

    Say who you are and a mini bio... keep it short, as people don't want to hear how brilliant you are, or how brilliant you think you are! Stay humble and "real" - you are not some sort of super human with a flawless and glorious track record with never an error or mistake in your past. Be real - don't be revisionist - give a mini bio but warts and all! But not too warty as you don't want people scratching their heads wondering why they are bothering to listen to you!

    Sketch out the presentation

    Again, give a short piece of what the presentation is about, what you seek to address and how it is relevant to the audience.

- **Humility**

    Be humble when speaking, you are just like everyone else. In reality, if you were to be honest, you are probably struggling with the very things that you are going to be talking about. The advice that you give is most likely the advice you need more than anyone. Therefore, convey that to the audience. Not to be conveyed in some sort of false humility, but a true humility that says that you are like everyone else – you have weaknesses, you have failings, you have successes and you are generally a mixed bag. You are no different than the person in the audience so let that be evident in what you say and how you say it.

Humility is not just what you say, it is your whole being. You have to avoid fake humility. Anyone can say "yeah, I'm not good at this either!" - but if the person speaking is not a humble person, then people will see right through this act. The audience will know - the talk may be humble in the narrative but the speaker in reality is not humble. Deep humility is the belief that you do not have all the answers...in fact you have very few. Deep humility is the consciousness that you are not perfect - you hold some truth but certainly not all of it and that you are very much a work in progress. And you must also convey that, as a work in progress, progression in any endeavour can rarely be achieved on your own as it always requires others. Humility then should just ooze out of you. You can't pretend to be humble, and you can't say stuff that sounds humble - everyone will get wise to it. The greatest entrepreneurs and the greatest leaders and the greatest people I have ever known are those who have deep humility. It's not seen in softly spoken, emotive words ...it's seen in the totality of the person, their life, their talk, their behaviour, their mannerisms and their treatment of others.

The humble speaker will naturally then strike a perfect balance of confidence in the subject matter and delivery, but by their words and behaviour they will portray humility. Too much humility and the audience may be wondering why they are listening to the person, but too little humility and the audience will see the speaker as an arrogant "know it all". The one with deep humility will not stray into either extreme.

- **Humour**

    Let humour come naturally. If humour ain't there, it just ain't there! I have said something off the cuff in a talk and people have laughed their leg off. I then thought "oh, that's a good line" and then said exactly the same, (what I thought a humorous line) to a different audience to be met with blank expressions and, can hear a pin drop, achingly painful silence - with the only one smiling being me with the hopeful anticipation of a similar response enjoyed previously. Let humour come naturally. Don't aim for laughs - you are not a comedy act! You are not the King of the one liners! Humour, if it comes, should come naturally like the weather - it will come in all forms with varying degrees of appeal and varying levels of response.

- **Walking the stage**

    There is a danger of walking around the stage as it can come across as misplaced arrogance. Indeed, conversely, by walking around the stage you may even look like you are nervous. And also in the middle of your talk, if you need your notes, you are potentially walking away from the notes and you could therefore look pretty ridiculous if you forget what to say. And yes, you will look ridiculous, if you forget what to say. Some may say "but everyone forgets their lines from time to time on stage" – and yes, they do - but it didn't stop them also looking ridiculous when they forgot their lines and had no notes to refer to!

    Some will get away with walking the stage, as it will just look and feel right that they are walking the stage. However, others will not get away with walking around the stage and it simply will just not look right. My gut feeling is to suggest that you don't walk around the stage. Instead, use your power of insight and conviction to animate your presentation and inspire and engage the audience instead of strutting around the stage!

HOW TO ENGAGE THE AUDIENCE!

I suspect that most speaker's objective, is to engage the audience. In other words, they want to have the audience's attention, their interest, their emotional, mental and intellectual participation. The speaker wants the audience to be "with" him or her. There are a number of factors to ensure the audience engages with you, the speaker.

RELEVANCE

The speaker, and what the speaker says, needs to be relevant to the audience. The key to success of anything is to be relevant. To be relevant in business, you have to have a product or service that provides a solution to a problem that exists in the market. The problem needs to be suffered by sufficient numbers of people or organisations, and the problem sufferers want a solution, and finally you can sell that solution to them at a price less than the cost of enduring the problem. And if you can do all of that and deliver an above average customer experience that is better than the competition – then you are relevant! You will be big time relevant!

And in the same way, the speaker has to be relevant. The speaker also has to provide a solution to the problem that the audience is suffering. There has to be many in the audience suffering that problem, they all must want a solution and the value they get must at least be more than the price of the ticket to attend the event. As a speaker, if you achieve this, and are relevant to the audience, then you will engage them.

QUESTIONS

Ask questions to the audience, and when asking the questions, make sure that you don't shoot someone down if they give you a stupid answer. Work with the audience, encourage them (never patronise them), and create an environment where people feel safe to contribute with dignity and respect.

EYE CONTACT

Eye contact is very important and can be difficult, particularly if you are nervous. When speaking publicly, it so often can be a challenge to know where to look when speaking to an audience. In any crowd of people, the temptation is to fix your eyes on the smiling head nodders. I love the smiling head nodders because they are the encouragers, the ones who keep you going - as opposed to the cynical looking person who looks like they are about to nod off!! However, thc temptation is to speak to either group exclusively. Be encouraged by the head nodder but don't ignore everyone else!! Balance your vision out…look a little to the left, to the centre, to the right, to the back and to the front! Always have a balance in eye contact.

And in keeping your eyes on the audience, look at people and not just their eyes but also their soul! Soul gazing can only come from someone who has deep conviction, huge amounts of empathy grounded in experience, and a desire to connect and help those who are listening. Soul gazing is difficult to master but it can be highly impactful for those on the receiving end - so try and master it!

WHAT DRINK ARE YOU SERVING?

Different drinks can affect us all so differently. My favourite drinks are milk and an energy drink! And both drinks impact on me in different ways. Milk is a good nourishing drink that is healthy and makes me feel really good. The energy drink is not that nourishing at all, gives me a momentary energy boost and then leaves me fairly tired and flat a couple of hours later. Anyway, when you are delivering a talk, what drink are you serving? In other words, how do you want people to feel? What do you want the effects of your talk to be on the listener? I suggest there are various drinks that can be served when delivering a talk?

THE ENERGY DRINK TALK

Your talk gives the audience an emotional boost for a few hours, very inspired and bursting with enthusiasm but the lack of substance ultimately will leave them feeling undernourished, leading them to probably forget what has been said and maybe even feeling a bit shortchanged and cynical.

THE SUGARY DRINK

This will leave people feeling happy, hyper and full of fizz! This may be absolutely fine because everyone needs these feelings from time to time. However, just remember that if you want to make real long lasting impact that changes people's lives for the better – you need to give them more than just sugar! They need real nourishment!

MILK

Apparently, milk is one of the most complete foods you can have. It has everything for body and mind and it nourishes the body in ways that sugary and/or caffeinated drinks can't. If you want your talk to have lasting impact on the listener and to strengthen them in areas where they may be weak - then deliver a talk that serves up milk. Nourish the listener with rich insights that will build them up and strengthen them for the challenges of tomorrow.

STYLE OVER SUBSTANCE

I actually am fairly relaxed about a talk that has little substance but a lot of style. However, at the end of the talk you have to be so inspired, so changed and so lifted that you feel you could walk on water! If there is not much style though, then there definitely has to be a great deal of substance with plenty of unique insights based on rich data and experiential understanding.

MAKE IT! THE "MAKE ITS" OF A PRESENTATION

- **Make it memorable**

   "The opposite of love is not hate, it's indifference."

   Elie Wiesel (holocaust survivor)

   The last thing you want is the audience to be indifferent to what you have said. One way or the other you want your talk to be memorable. How you make it memorable is up to you, but prepare and deliver the talk with a mindset and a goal to make it one that people will be remembering and indeed talking about for some time to come! Having a talk that is memorable will be achieved in a number of different ways. It may be memorable by just the style of delivery, humour, or the richness of insight and depth into the subject matter. It may be memorable for the wrong reasons (remember the "go low, go slow, go …I don't know" guy), so just make sure that it is memorable for all the right reasons!

- **Make it measurable**

    Qualitative information is good but don't forget the quantitative. Sometimes your narrative needs to be backed up by some good reliable statistics and numbers. The talk may not need to have lots of data but it is always good, where relevant, to just hit the audience with some numbers from really good, strong authoritative sources.

- **Make it meaningful**

    Your talk needs to have a point and it needs to be relevant to the audience – otherwise; what is the point! Meaningfulness in your talk will come from it being relevant to the audience, but also that it is delivered with heart and a depth that clearly displays to everyone that everything you say you actually really and truly believe in it and …mean it! Therefore, conviction, strong belief and deep understanding of what you are talking about are all necessary, if you are to make your talk meaningful.

- **Make it magical**

  A magical talk is a talk that goes beyond just being meaningful. A magical talk is something really special. This is a talk that changes people, that impacts on them so significantly that patterns and practices of their lives start to change. The talk maybe brings them to tears or makes them confront themselves in ways that they have not done before. Magical talks can lead people to set up a business that they never thought they would or could do. It can lead people to change their attitudes, it can bring people to new ways of thinking, and it may even cause people to change the direction of their careers and indeed lives! Magical talks are rare but they can be powerful and life changing, and if you have had the privilege to hear one of these talks, then you will understand what I mean. A magical talk will most likely be filled with stories, illustrations and an engagement with the audience that goes beyond the average. It is always good to set your targets high – so aim for delivering a magical talk!

PAINT PICTURES

There are many people who think pictorially. They need images to make sense of what you are saying and importantly, to be *engaged* with what you are saying. You may show these images visually or you may simply paint pictures in people's minds. The way to do this is through illustrations. Illustrations can sometimes sound a bit forced, a bit fake, a bit taken from a book on illustrations! Therefore, as with humour, only use it if it comes naturally, if the illustrations are real life and preferably happened to you or individuals that most of us can identify with. In a sermon once, I was talking about the need to rely on the strength of God and not on our own strength. I said in the sermon that if we try to rely on our own strength, we will typically not make it and will fall every time, but if we trust in God for His strength, then He will get us through. The illustration I used was from a time when I was water-skiing with the family.

The water ski instructor had been telling this guy how to water-ski successfully without falling straight into the water. He told him to hold onto the rope, keep his knees bent and arms straight and hold that position. Then the instructor said that when the speed boat powers off, don't try to get up out of the water on your own strength and don't try and lift yourself up. The instructor said to him that when the motor boat starts moving and gathering speed, just keep your arms straight and knees bent and the power of the boat will lift you out of the water without the guy needing to pull himself up. Of course, this guy didn't listen, and every time the boat started to move and speed up, the guy trying to water-ski kept trying to lift himself out of the water on his own strength. And of course, he kept falling smack into the water! This continued until he gave up!

However, my eight-year-old daughter Emily, was told the exact same thing as she got into the water and put her water skis on. The instructor said to Emily - "keep your knees bent Emily, and arms straight and when the boat starts to move and speed up, just hold your position and let the power of the boat lift you up out of the water...don't try and get up out of the water on your own strength." Of course, and I would say this, my daughter obeyed every word the instructor said, and as this mighty speed boat powered off and gathered speed, my little daughter kept her knees bent and arms straight and relied totally on the power of the boat to lift her up out of the water. She didn't try and get up on her own strength, she relied on the strength and power of the boat. And within seconds she was water-skiing!

Most people can visualise this in their mind, they may never have water-skied, but they understand what is involved and they can easily have a picture in their mind. There was a fundamental truth that had been taught about dependence on the strength of God but it could be remembered and applied by the listener by recalling the story of my little daughter on water skis!

Therefore, paint pictures to better explain something, reinforce a point or encourage the audience to remember what you have said.

TELL TRUE STORIES

This is an obvious point but if you want to inspire an audience, then tell them inspirational things! And the most inspirational things to hear are stuff that has actually happened! Don't tell stories that are fake or downloaded from the internet! Tell stories that are real. And also, tell stories that most people will have never heard of – in other words, you are giving people something unique. The Churchill stories will have been heard by many, or the stories of football legend x or soldier y are also likely to have been heard. Try to avoid the usual predictable stuff that most people will have heard or picked up on at some stage in their life. The best stories are personal ones or ones that others will definitely not have heard of before.

One of the inspirational stories I shared from my other book "Start to Grow", and I have shared it publicly too, is the story about my father. The following is an extract from "Start to Grow" on my inspirational story about my dad...

"It was 20 January 1990, and I was looking out over the city from the penthouse suite of one of the most famous hotels in the world. Celebrating your thirteenth birthday in such opulent surroundings, was the privilege of being the son of one of the company directors that owned this hotel at that time. As I lay in the Jacuzzi bath, taking a sip of something non-alcoholic that I had sneaked from the minibar, I decided, in that moment, that running a business was what I wanted to do with my life; if it gave you this type of lifestyle, then that was the career that I wanted. This was fun and would enable me to do things that others could only dream of.

For two years, I experienced going from one hotel to another, one penthouse suite to the next, as my father immersed himself, and my family, into this hotelier world. My father loved business but particularly relished the challenge of making deals. Business was never primarily about the money for my father. He was in it for the excitement of building and creating something great that others could be part of and enjoy. This was the man who was not only my father but someone who inspired me, the man who I looked up to. Needless to say, as a young boy in his teens, life was great.

However, things were about to change because around that time, we were in the middle of the recession of the early 1990s; the economy was contracting and interest rates more or less doubled overnight, putting huge strain on businesses, but that was to be the least of our problems.

Within six months, I was in my bedroom struggling to load a game onto my 1980s computer (two hours in those days), when my mother entered the room. I remember it like it was yesterday. With a few words my world changed forever. My father was on a business trip to North America and he had rung to say he had been taken into hospital. He had been diagnosed with leukemia. Life as we knew it crashed down. My father's battles had just begun. In the midst of being treated for his illness and dealing with great physical pain, the recession hit the hotelier world hard and his business collapsed too. This was what my father described as 'the lowest point in his life'.

Within a few months, through much prayer, he defied the medical world and found himself in remission. He had made it through; he was alive and he was well, but he was practically broke. He had a family that had to be financially supported and had to find a way to earn an income. Incredibly, the optimistic negotiator, the drive of the entrepreneur, rose to the surface again. He got up and went out in search of a new deal.

Doing deals is not easy. They can be complex and demanding, but for my father dealmaking was an art, a pleasure, something to be enjoyed and savoured, the beginning of an adventure, the promise of fun and the hope of something new and challenging. However, his finest deal, his masterpiece, was about to be put into action. As he strolled into the empty offices of what was once his great empire, he picked up the phone and rang one of the largest restaurant chains in the world. What he said, I don't know. How he pulled it off is a mystery, but I was soon to find out that Pizza Hut was coming to Northern Ireland! The phoenix had risen from the ashes in the form of bread, cheese and tomatoes.

The launch of the first Pizza Hut in Northern Ireland was in Carryduff, ironically where our business, ShredBank, is based today. I can still remember the huge smile on my father's face on launch night. He was back. He had conquered the great challenges he had faced and he had found a way to make a success.

Within less than two years of that night, my father sadly passed away. Before he died, he had five Pizza Huts established, had given us a great life during that time, generated an income and ensured that after his death my mum would be looked after financially.

The point of the story for me and hopefully for others, is that success is possible even in the most difficult of personal and economic circumstances. The world may be in chaos, the economy may be flatlining but there are hundreds and thousands of businesses that succeed every day. It amazes me that even during calamitous times people still succeed, people still do business. I remember as a child watching the Gulf War on the television, seeing cities flattened and businesses bombed and yet, the following day when you would watch the news again, you would see commercial vans and cars on the road, continuing to trade even when their world was literally falling apart. I remember going with my father to Pizza Hut in Bangor one Sunday morning and seeing the destruction after a bomb had gone off that morning. Incredibly, local businessmen and women were getting to work (with the usual local banter) restoring their premises, ready to do business, and determined to be successful.

The view that 'success is possible' is a mindset change that is fundamentally important to your business. In a sense, you realise that no matter what happens in the world, no matter what happens in the economy, you can make your business successful. Without the realisation that you can succeed, without that change from a negative mindset to a positive one, you won't do it. Your business strategy will be short-term, it will be in survival mode and your business will never survive in the medium and long term. Many businesses, both local and international, started during challenging economic times and survived not just one, but many recessions throughout their corporate history. Not only did they survive, but they also grew their businesses to become successful local and global brands. ShredBank started during the beginning of the global credit crisis that ultimately led to a global recession. We started from scratch during this financial climate, but, despite this, we were able to create and grow a shredding business that has become a multi-award winning company and a great local brand."

TALK KILLERS

These are some talk killers that I have learnt from brutal experience:

- **Jokes that don't work are talk killers** - so, stop trying to be a comedian!

- **Questions that aren't answered** – avoid this by asking ones that are answerable and don't ask complex questions!

- **The audience gets bored and you don't see it** – avoid this by opening your eyes and see the mood of the people and adapt accordingly!

- **Forgetting what to say** - this is a killer so always take notes! None of this go low, go slow, don't know nonsense!!!!

- **You are not relevant** - wrap up, learn from it and make sure you read the section on pre-event preparation!

- **Difficult question from a difficult person** - there always will be one who will ask a difficult question or like the sound of his or her own voice. You need to work with them, agree with them, worship them and basically do whatever you need to do to shut them up. But don't go head to head with them – that's a disaster right there!!

- **Not being able to answer a question** - don't get flustered and spoof and try to evade or give a naff answer. Just say " I have no idea" or "great question but you have got me" or "hey, let's open this one to the floor ...who can shed light on this one?" By doing this you are showing that you have humility, that you have a lot of answers but not all of them, and it also involves the audience in the reality of that and will no doubt help them to engage.

- **Some aspects of your appearance** - you may have, as a guy, your zip down (disaster), you may have a clump of gel visible on your hair (I have this removed by my wife often) or some stain on your shirt or blouse, or some makeup error (I'm a guy - what do I know) but the key thing is to do a full mirror check before you take to the stage. Whatever you say and no matter how good you are...it will all die if you have an ink mark on your cheek or your zip down!

- **Overdressing or underdressing** - you need to largely fit with the audience and occasion. You could stand out a bit and dress differently but just be careful - make a good judgement call on this.

THINGS TO AVOID

- **Avoid clichés.** Clichés like – *"the best of men are only men at best,"* *"think outside of the box"*... *"Punch above your weight"*.. I have said them many times but they are so unoriginal, and actually don't really mean anything to the listener.

- **Credibility crisis.** Only talk about something you really understand and that you could, within reason, field any question.

- **Excessive sweating.** Hydrate before and during the talk, try to pace yourself and not be overly animated in your talk and use plenty of antiperspirant.

- **Excessive hand movement.** I sometimes have my hands going like a windmill! It's just me and it may just be you – that's ok! Just be conscious of it and try to keep a good balance between hand movement and a less animated approach.

- **Going past your time limit.** Good preparation will reduce this problem but avoid asking someone to make a "T" sign with their hands 5 minutes before you are supposed to finish your talk and then every minute after your talk is supposed to be finished. Daft "T" signs are very irritating and distracting!

- **Forgetting your lines.** After much learning and preparation, make sure you always have notes!

- **Boring the audience.** Your journey may actually not be that interesting so talk about more interesting journeys experienced by others! Some of your life stories that give illustrations may be fine but if your profile is weak, your brand is non-existent, and your life stories are a bit "meat and potatoes", then I suggest you talk about other people's stories rather than your own.

- **Being Fake.** Avoid being overly animated, avoid dramatic pauses, avoid fake emotion (I heard a pastor had on his notes "start to cry at this point"!), avoid fake outcries of sentimentality or righteous indignation, avoid fake theatrics to appeal to people's emotions. Just be genuine and real – not disingenuous and fake!

GIVE PEOPLE A ROAD MAP TO SUCCESS

People are inspired not just by how you make them feel, the inspirational stories that you tell them, and by conveying a deep sense that failure happens to us all and there is a way out – but they are also inspired by seeing clearly the direction that they now must go. People need to have a road map for success. As discussed before, the audience or the listener(s) have come with a problem that they are suffering, they are surrounded potentially by others who are also suffering that problem, and they do want a solution to that problem that they are suffering. And therefore, you will give your talk and it will inform, it will guide, it will tell stories, it will entertain and all of that good stuff. However, sustaining that inspiration for the listener can only be achieved if you actually lay out the things that they must do, or consider, in order to address that problem that they are suffering! Otherwise, they may leave your talk inspired, but in a week's time when they are still struggling with the problem and feeling somewhat directionless, they just might lose a bit of that inspirational magic that they had enjoyed when you were on stage.

Therefore, whether you are talking about digital marketing, selling, business growth or gardening…set out the road map for making things right and solving the problems that they have. Make the points actionable and memorable and value-adding. This will ensure they are able to take all that inspirational noise and make real tangible beneficial changes to themselves or their business.

SOME FINAL TIPS...

- Practice your talk to death so that you "own it" and could say it in your sleep (talk to the wall a lot!)

- Avoid all jargon or clichés.

- Tell them a little about what "they know they know", a lot about what "they know they don't know", and a massive amount of what they "don't know they don't know".

- Make it relevant ...make it real...talk in everyday language.

- Empathise with them.

- Every slide/point must be "adding value to them" and it will make a tangible benefit to their business – it must pass the "so what test!"

- At times frighten them, at times encourage them and at times make them think.

- Only use humour if you are humorous.

- Eye contact with everyone, engage them and interact.

- Clichés, jargon, business talk, health and wealth message... Avoid them all.

- Authority comes not by tone of voice, or pitch, or waving hands around but by your command of the subject matter. That will give you all the authority you need.

- Let yourself go a bit, and talk with conviction but above all – be YOU.

GIVE THEM A MESSAGE OF HOPE

Inspiration comes from a message of hope. People don't get inspired by listening to a messenger of doom and despair. And yes, of course, there is much to despair about in the world that we live in today but equally there is much cause for hope. Therefore, if you want to inspire others then give them a reason to hope. Your talk should include stories of hope, strategies of hope, examples of hope, and an overall message that there is hope…there is always hope!

ABOUT THE AUTHOR

Philip Bain, graduated with a First Class Honours degree in Business Studies from Ulster University, and became the youngest Marketing Manager at that time at the age of 22. He was awarded the Business Leader of Tomorrow Award by Lord Sainsbury in 2002 and has since gone on to win Entrepreneur of the Year 2010, Young Business person 2011 and also won the Nectar Business Award in 2012 presented by Karren Brady from "The Apprentice."

Having been involved in growing and developing six start-up companies, Philip set up ShredBank in 2007 with his friend and business partner James Carson. It grew rapidly despite the recession and became the largest on-site shredding company in Northern Ireland. Winning twelve awards and becoming an Investors in People Gold Organisation, ShredBank is a local company that has become a world-class organisation.

Philip has a wealth of experience in leadership in the private sector, social economy and faith-based organisations. Philip was formerly Chairman of the Chartered Management Institute in Northern Ireland, Chairman of the Institute of Consultants, on the Council of the Northern Ireland Chamber of Commerce, a Council

Member of The Prince's Trust in Northern Ireland and a Visiting Professor of Ulster University and on the Business Advisory Board of Enactus in Ulster University and Queen's University.

In 2020, Philip is a regular speaker on the subjects of business growth and entrepreneurship. For over ten years, Philip has delivered seminars and training to literally thousands of people and hundreds of organisations including enterprise agencies, universities, colleges, councils and private companies. He has delivered leadership training to a number of Northern Ireland's largest businesses and is currently a mentor to many entrepreneurs and business owners. A committed Christian, Philip is a lay preacher and currently preaches in churches across the province.

He is the author of Amazon best seller "Start to Grow" and "Start to Lead." These books have been sold across the world and in particular the UK, North America and Asia.

Lightning Source UK Ltd.
Milton Keynes UK
UKHW010827201021
392517UK00001B/13